# DIANE WAKOSKI

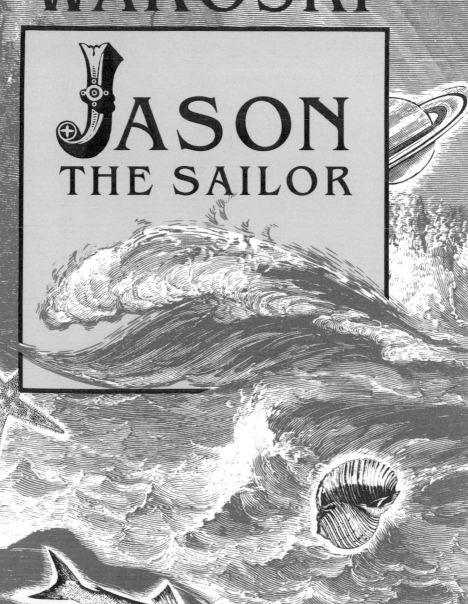

# JASON
## THE SAILOR

Diane Wakoski

# The Archaeology of Movies and Books

Volume I: Medea the Sorceress
Volume II: Jason the Sailor

## By Diane Wakoski

*Coins & Coffins* (1962)
*Four Young Lady Poets* (1962)
*Discrepancies and Apparitions* (1966)
*The George Washington Poems* (1967)
*Inside the Blood Factory* (1968)
*The Magellanic Clouds* (1970)
*The Motorcycle Betrayal Poems* (1971)
*Smudging* (1972)
*Dancing on the Grave of a Son of a Bitch* (1973)
*Trilogy: Coins & Coffins, Discrepancies and Apparitions,*
    *The George Washington Poems* (1974)
*The Wandering Tattler* (1975)
*Virtuoso Literature for Two and Four Hands* (1975)
*Waiting for the King of Spain* (1976)
*The Man Who Shook Hands* (1978)
*Trophies* (1979)
*Cap of Darkness* (1980)
*The Magician's Feastletters* (1982)
*The Collected Greed, Parts 1-13* (1984)
*The Rings of Saturn* (1986)
*Emerald Ice: Selected Poems 1962-1987* (1988)
*Medea the Sorceress* (1991)
*Jason the Sailor* (1993)

# DIANE WAKOSKI

# JASON
# THE SAILOR

BLACK SPARROW PRESS · SANTA ROSA · 1993

Poems in this collection have appeared in: *ACM, Caliban, Cat's Ear, Cream City Review, Louisiana Literature, Manoa, Negative Capability, Nota, Paintbrush, Rain City Review, Red Cedar Review, River Styx, Stiletto 2, UCSD Newsletter, Way Station.*

Excerpts from *Quantum Reality: Beyond the New Physics* by Nick Herbert, copyright © 1985 by Nick Herbert. Used by permission of Doubleday, a division of Bantam Doubleday Dell Publishing Group, Inc.

Black Sparrow Press books are printed on acid-free paper.

LIBRARY OF CONGRESS CATALOGING-IN-PUBLICATION DATA
Wakoski, Diane.
    Jason the Sailor / Diane Wakoski.
      p.      cm. — (The Archaeology of movies and books ; v. 2)
    ISBN 0-87685-903-1 : $25.00. — ISBN 0-87685-902-3 (pbk.) : $13.00. —
ISBN 0-87685-904-X (signed cloth ed.) : $30.00
    I. Title.     II. Series: Wakoski, Diane. Archaeology of movies and books ; v. 2.
PS3573.A42J37     1993
811'.54—dc20                                  93-740
                                                        CIP

This book is for Steel Man and all the Troubadours
who sing to me

# TABLE OF CONTENTS

# JASON THE SAILOR

Here's how to change the past. Using conventional optics, bring the two beams together that have traveled right or left of the focusing galaxy and allow them to cross. Now decide (quantum meter option) whether to put your photon-sensitive phosphor screen at intersection A or at a later position B after the beams have separated. For each photon, you can take one of these measurement options but not both. If you choose position A, you observe wave interference effects, indicating that the photon took both paths, and it is even possible to estimate the relative time delay between paths from the shape of this interference pattern.

Nick Herbert, *Quantum Reality: Beyond the New Physics*

# BLUE SUEDE SHOES

The blond whose skin was translucent as a glass slipper,
    whose small-boned frame allowed silk to drape
    as if underwater crenellating fans of sea anemone
    were breathing when she walked,
wore a sapphire blue maternity dress
and sat in the living room of The Home for Unwed Mothers
playing cards with her less-glamorous enceinte friends.

I sat on the sofa, reading Shakespeare's love sonnets, or
    was it
*Tess of the D'Urbervilles*? 1956. Pasadena, California.
Most of us there are teenagers.
Though she's a beauty;
I'm the book-worm brain. And I heard her say,
    that blond, the girl who'd been to a party with a
    college fraternity boy and wound up here,
    as ashamed as all the rest of us
        like the nurse who found out she was going to
           have
        the hydrocephalic baby fathered by her hospital
        boss who was married to someone else,
        the fourteen-year-old raped by her father,
        and lots of girls like me whose boyfriends loved us
        (we thought),
        but were not ready to be fathers,
she who wore a diamond on one of her sea cucumber

pale fingers and always had a cool
remark on her witty red tongue, said
    "This baby will probably be born with blue
        suede shoes."
I imagined her blond baby boy,
    a princeling, with royal
        Cupid lips and his mother's
           nose, straight as a golden pin;
             he'd be a blue blood,
        I thought. A king in baby shoes.
My literary ear recognized a title, though I knew little else,
listening to Beethoven or Chopin as I did,
not even the Beach Boys, now such a classic sound to me,
    representing the Orange County of my youth,
    of beach parties, and parked cars, and
    high school class rings.
I hadn't heard of Carl Perkins who wrote the song before
    Elvis
recorded it, though I knew
    where Memphis was; hadn't heard of
        Sun Studios, or "The King,"
the Sun King, I thought; Incas, blood sacrifices, virgins
having their hearts cut out over jungle pyramids.
    I knew that royalty was in my blood,
my swollen belly, and I knew that my love,
like that love alluded to in the sonnet,
was the kind
that was so great
that I'd "scorn to trade it" for a kingdom.
I felt the martyrdom of adolescence, but was
reminded over and over, by the delicate princess face
    of the woman who fantasized that her
        taboo baby might be born with little blue suede
           Elvis-shoes on his blond feet,
that I was the brain,

she, the beauty,
and Chance had us both sitting here in the same parlor,
glass slippers shattered,
        bare foot and pregnant.

No, no, no,
that wasn't us!

There *were* shoes. If not for us
        Cinderella's crystal slipper. Or Dorothy,
        innocent Dorothy, drug addict Dorothy's ruby
        slippers of Oz,
                            then there were
for our sons,
those swinging blue suede shoes;
and we would be left with music,
music in our heads, both of us,
she listening to Elvis
and I to the mad dissonant sounds of late Beethoven.
She with her skin translucent as a glass slipper
and I with my shy-girl skin, blushing, blushed ruby-slipper
        red,
    both of us dancing, bare footed, just dancing,
            red glass and blue suede shoes,
        to survive our shame.

On the other hand, if you put the phosphor screen at location
B you see that each photon takes only one path, either left or
right of the galactic lens. In our imagination we can picture
this particular photon traveling partnerless for eons, because
today we chose to do experiment B instead of experiment A.

You can make the next photon take both paths by quickly choosing the other measurement option. By our choice of what we look at today we seem to be able to change a photon's attribute acquired billions of years before we were born.

Wheeler's delayed-choice experiment seems to show that the past is not fixed but alters according to present decisions. Popular philosopher Alan Watts reports that certain Eastern philosophies have come to a similar conclusion concerning the creative power of the present tense: "The moment of the world's creation is seen to lie, not in some unthinkably remote past, but in the eternal now."

Note that our ability to change the past is limited. We can indeed choose whether each quantum entity becomes a one-path or a two-path photon, but we cannot select where the two-path photon will fall in the interference pattern or which path the one-path photon will take.

Nick Herbert, *Quantum Reality: Beyond the New Physics*

---

The Rose Diner

Dear Craig,

Sometimes I think of you, and all the young troubadours to whom I sing, for whom I write letters or act out my life, as taking the place of the Jason who left me when I was young. Maybe if I can tell you my story, it will change something, perhaps not

17

the past, but the future? Maybe I wouldn't have to get old, or to die? Maybe I won't have to lose my lover, my son, husband or father? I don't know.
I do know that my story has been focused on men, not women, and when I talk of my "penis envy," I continually think of how I have loved men more than myself, and wanted their love, though since I myself do not love women, have never quite understood why men should love me. What a set-up I was for all the Jasons I loved to sail away from me. I am not sure why I think this could ever change, but I guess my whole story is about wanting men to love women as much as women love men.

Yr Lady of the Sea

DW

## FEAR OF WOMEN

My mother's secret was small:
        her few women friends —
barely noticed like those wispy tissue-flowered branches
of Baby's Breath that filament wedding bouquets —
        as solitary as the spiders I found making webs
        in the orange grove where I lived.
        Marion like a Scotty dog, with her razor-cut bob,
        square-hipped and shouldered, tractor-like body

18

who when I was a precocious ten suggested
that I might love a book called
*The Well of Loneliness.* And Mickey
who lived with her mother and father though
she was thirty-five, tall and rangy like a golden retriever,
had a whiskey voice,
and once took us to visit California eccentrics
who intriguingly told my sister and me
that they always ate their dessert first,
only ate other food if they still had room/they served us
fresh strawberry shortcake and whipped cream
(new blood on fresh snow) as we sat in their trailer
on the desert and talked about psychics.

Southern California women, I thought. They
smoked, were divorced, had deep voices
and seemed glad they had
no children. Helen, the woman from
     a newspaper ad, who was little and stubborn,
     like a wire-haired terrier,
     moved in with us
     just after the Depression,
     and slept in the same sofa bed with our mother.
     I hated her and laughed when she hit her head on a
cupboard door one day, cruel little five-year-old that I was.
     She went away after trying to teach me to make
     perfect embroidery stitches
     which I never mastered. It never
occurred to me to wonder about these solitary,
odd women who were
my mother's few and unsuccessful friends
until this year when I walked into a bookstore
and saw in the Women's section under the designation
     "Lesbian Novels"

that volume whose title I had remembered all these years,
        though
never been curious enough to read.

I always knew my fear of men and night,
of the heavy-boughed trees weighted with golden fruit,
came from my mother's sexual failures with her husband,
that Jason in Naval uniform
I grew up longing for;
but here is yet another facet of my
childlife to blame her for:
        my fear of women which has never made it possible
        for me to even want
        a woman as a friend.
                        How well I learned and feared the sound
of coyotes, barking like dogs in the hills above the orange
        trees,
while I longed only for the ocean
of my Daddy's sailor love. All the while
the groves at night frightened
me with rustling leaves
                        dark as dried blood,
with rustling
        spider web-embroidered leaves,
leaves like dog's muddy paw prints,
            with razor-bobbed, strawberry-shortcake,
                    cigarette-breathed leaves,
the rustling of witches who might prevent my father from
        returning
home, might come any time
and steal my baby breath away.

                                    The Rose Diner
                                    Los Angeles

Dear Craig,

Oh, I am haunted by my father, the sailor, and my
mother, the bookkeeper, who is more Medusa than
Medea. Being scorned by my father for another
woman turned my mother's naturally rigid personality
into bitter stone, so I guess logically she would not
be the Medusa but a victim of that snaky power. All
these years I've thought of myself as Medea, my
father as the original Jason. I guess I mistakenly left
my mother out of the equation. So many Jasons, so
many Medeas. The Medeas turn into Medusas. And
all those barking dogs.

Yr Lady of Desert Light,

DW

## MEDUSA IN THE CITY DUMP

Oh, what did they mean —
she had snakes for hair? What did they mean?
Cobras rising up to the full height of a man,
ready to strike? The python sliding down the tree trunk

21

over his head in a hiss of coils which suddenly
wrap a man's chest, constrict his breathing?

I found you lying in the dump just outside of town,
your nylon hair standing like porcupine quills ready to
        shoot out
at the barking dog.
Your eyes do look surprised, I think.
You discarded doll, whom some little girl
        got for Christmas, probably once advertised on TV,
        wearing a dress of spangles, red white and blue,
        like the one a sorceress wrapped around a princess
        to burn her to death for female treachery
your eyes so round, one half closed, as if to hide the fact
the other one might be a bullet hole.

They called the priestesses, who sat down in the crevices
of the earth at Delphi and smoked out their oracles,
"Pythoness," from the snake-dragon the boy Apollo killed
but surely remembering the image of baby Herakles
his cherubic muscled miniature-man arms, wrestling
two snakes and killing them in his crib. You don't have
pythons or vipers like black whips for hair.
Only this stiff nylon, unbending when everything
else about you is melting and soft with age.

Why do I see all the power of female
in this discarded doll, lying on the sodden carton
        from a water heater and a rusty tank of
        what must have been
        the old boiler the new one replaced?
Why are women
only powerful when they are old
or discarded, when their doll eyes

are still slightly beautiful with paint
and they are missing the skin of youth?

Because they are no longer women?
Because at last they have been transformed?
Their snaky power, so long coiled in the brain,
now shooting out of the head, into stiff tangles,
frozen like the locks of this doll?

Not even old yet,
                    I've had my head shorn
in anticipation of what age brings.
I'm no longer Rapunzel,
though I still live
in the same tower,
and I still look down at the Prince
who says he will
rescue me if I can just offer him
some way
to do it. My long hair, the coils of braid or brain
I once could have thrown down—they were starting to rise,
stiffening like the quills of a porcupine when the dogs
        had started
getting too close, and I felt them turning into cobras,
        rising up
every time my name was mentioned without respect,
                    "She's a real dog,"/"She's a snake,"
or elongating into the one great thrust of python
shooting down the trunk to squeeze the foolish hunter
to death. Soft glinted strands of my shiny hair
fall to the floor every month now, as I am cut into
        an elegant
shape. If hair grows after you're dead,
I suppose I'll revert. Dig me up, and you'll see

Medusa, as many snakes as you'd find on an Indiana Jones
        movie set,
coiling and quarreling around my rotting face.

But now, though I know I am just like this doll
lying on the heap of refuse in the city dump, I'll hide it,
as well as I can. It is my power. You don't need to look
        at it:
or worry about being turned to stone, as you once might
        have had to.
I still cling to this Hollywood *Pretty Woman* world,
        though I
have no hope of rescue from my tower. I'll keep
the snakes inside;
you can look at me, without mirror or sword.

And those dogs—
    a reminder that Rapunzel and the witch
    were always one and the same.
The dogs—
    when you hear them, you'll know
    they're just guarding the place I live,
        though I suppose that's why I still scare you so much.

---

One thing has not changed. I never hear of any female high
rollers, and I presume they do not exist. I don't even know
if they would be welcome. In Vegas, women have never been
thought of as gamblers. They have always been something
else.

Alan Richman, "Lost Vegas"

---

24

The Rose Diner
Los Angeles

Dear Craig,

There is no way that I could ever turn to women for comfort or pleasure or nourishment. Certainly not for sex, love or romance. My little girl life in Southern California, lived primarily with my mother, my sister, my aunts, my mother's few women friends oppressed me. It convinced me that the world of men must be enchanted, beautiful. I found an accurate description of my response to the world of women in Camille Paglia's *Sexual Personae.* This response is what has made me so willing to search for and follow beautiful men.

---

Dionysus, god of fluids, rules a murky no man's land of matter half turned to liquid. Neumann notes the linguistic connection in German between *Mutter,* mother; *Moder,* bog; *Moor,* fen; *Marsch,* marsh; and *Meer,* ocean. A chthonian miasma hangs over woman, like the polluted cloud raining pestilence on Oedipus' Thebes. The miasma is woman's procreative fate, linking her to the primeval. Artemis is woman on the run,

breaking out of her cloud into Apollonian sunlight. Artemis'
radiance is a militant self-hardening, a refusal of menarche.
Dionysus, endorsing woman, also keeps her in the chthonian
swamp . . . In nature's female womb-world, there are no ob-
jects and no art.

Camille Paglia, *Sexual Personae*

---

Of course you know, Craig, that one of my obses-
sions is the longing for physical, seductive beauty, and
how entitled to it I feel, while always feeling not
quite successful. This image of eternal youth and
healthy beauty, or the search for it, hovers around all
my California girl mythology, my image of myself as
Diane, the moon woman, who is more silver than
gold.

I was brought up in a female world, and actually felt
very restricted by it. I grew up with only a mother
and sister, my father gone most of the time. I lived in
an isolated world and felt very deprived of male
culture. I have always idealized men, male culture,
and anything that shows men loving and caring for
women because this was left out of my childhood.
The result is not that I wanted to be a man but that
I wanted a man or men to love me.

# THE SEA

When we lived at the house in the orange grove
where black and yellow spiders bejeweled
the porch, my father, the sailor, played cribbage with us,
after breakfast, my little sister and me.

But there were only a few of those mornings.
The ruler-like board in which we pegged our
tallies also seemed to measure
the time he'd be
with us; the slick cards
in our bacon hands
must have pleased him, these two little eggs, his chicks,
and the way we could count,
        our bookkeeper-mother's children, California fruit,
        like the navel oranges outside the screen door,
but not enough. He never stayed long,
and then he was gone for good.
Dry as toast, our man-less lives
without Daddy, and breakfast still
my favorite meal, the smell of coffee,
the slightly greasy pack of cards we'd get out
after we'd wiped the oil-cloth table,
big and little sailor hands
dealing the cribbage game.

I don't have any particular attraction for goddess cults, and certainly chthonic mythology, which is ancient and very female, is not a primary source of my own personal myths. It is not images of motherhood or fertility which attract me, and those are at the center of ancient female mythology. I love the cool Athena, who is androgynous and as beautiful as a boy. I love the Diana who is a huntress with her silver bow and arrows. I love Medea who is a beautiful woman, a sorceress, and gives up her children when their father betrays her.

What a story I have to tell: how my longing turns Jason and Medea into twin halves of each other. How Jason belongs to Medea and has no right to another woman. How Medea turns into the Medusa. Oh, give me back the girl with the silver ankle.

Yr Sorceress in exile,

DW

## SILVER ARROWS

When I turn on the phone machine to listen
to our messages, his voice
is there,

narrow, hooded eyes,
    skiing the powdery slopes.
How brave, asking me
    to have a cup of coffee.
Can the old quicksilver tongue
    become Diana?
He might
    be shy as a deer but he
    need not run away.
He might ski
    arrow-like long arcs
    over whiteness,
    my frosty voice condensed
    into the mountain where
he might
    change the old story;
    oh, how can you change a story
    you don't yet know?

# THE EVOLUTION OF MORNING

The clean linen smell of the hot iron on cloth,
smoothing it like calla lilics
and a sound which I couldn't then
identify in the little house
in the orange grove with my mother
pressing the clothes
of girls and women—
    it was morning doves, their voice rattling in their throats,

and the little cooing sound they uttered as they fed
and then flew up, as a flock, off the ground.
That comes to me, when I say "morning"
But little else.
I don't remember mornings
when I was young, except that I hated to rise,
wanted to remain asleep and when I awakened, longed to
remain in bed
reading, or daydreaming.

Life was not much to me,
so much less vivid or entertaining
than books. "No imagination," she said,
"you have no
imagination." This is true, I can't even
fantasize things I know
could never happen,
so I don't dream, for instance, of movie
stars, taking me to bed, making love to me. Instead,
I dream of myself
as a teenager, being seduced and loved
by boys of the past,
who perhaps do resemble

Tom Cruise, John Cusack,
the ones with eyes.

The boy I dreamed so much about in 8th and 9th grades,
a big, blond, sturdy Irishman, built more like a football
          player.
Maybe
he was even on the team, how I lost track studying for
          college,
and thinking cashmere sweater thoughts about
myself. These new teenagers

who draw me into a magic theater
of identification with the young. I don't dream
of winning the lotto, or even of my husband
winning it. I dream that I am young again
and can do it all over, and recently
I started dreaming
of the young men I know as my children
accomplishing the tasks at which
I have failed.

Memory might be
imagination, or is it only
a substitute for one? I've bragged about
my eidetic memory, about the perfect recall
that started fading when my hands began to wrinkle
        and spot.
Mind is protoplasm too.
This winter turn, where the mists are rising up from the
dark ground, in steamy breaths, just like the coffee
        evaporating
upward
from its morning cup offers me whispers from the Pythoness.
She was right,
I never had any imagination. There was only
memory. But perhaps I've always had a Shadow Self.
Not Coyote, The Western Trickster,
but Medea, the Sorceress.
Not the memory of White Princess Privilege
which set me to longing on those mornings
when my mother ironed starched cotton dresses.
The betrayed lover
driving her chariot of dragons away
from California, the land of beautiful women.

Mornings are now the only time
when I can breathe, when I rise to my full height,
when I can make love to anyone.
When I can beguile myself,
or trick myself
into believing there is no death.

---

# FULL MOON EYES

*I think I could turn and live with animals, they are
so placid and self-contain'd,
I stand and look at them long and long.*

Walt Whitman, "Song of Myself"

It isn't that I didn't want to like you;
I always wanted
to like you, because in your cowboy hat
and torn jeans and with your very polite, almost cowboy
        polite
manners to me
                "Yes, ma'am,"
you were
likable. But I didn't want to
feel the way I do,
that those eyes which are almost like
girls' eyes, like flowers, like horses' eyes maybe,
        as seen by Jim Wright,

which looked straight at me with such belladonna innocence,
no macho challenge or even that kind of cool
or contained gaze I expect from handsome
men—I didn't want to feel
as if I could fall into them, as into a well,
or an abandoned mine shaft, and be lost. It's not
love; it's definitely not what I feel for my husband, or what
       I felt
for my first lover or the Motorcycle Betrayer or for any man
       I can
think of,
that strangely long procession through my life. It is not
       what
I would feel either, if I were your mother, something I
       cannot
even imagine.

Sometimes I think when you walk into the room
that it is an actor playing the part of someone with your
       name,
and I realize I have no idea if you exist, but then you say
       something,
and I look up into those eyes, yes, as if I were looking
       up at some
racehorse,
such a different piece of flesh than I am,
and as Whitman says he could turn and be with animals,
and as he too thinks particularly of the thorough
bred stallion, I don't find myself mesmerized either. Just
       standing
there,
rather like Whitman I think,
admiring something,
being drawn into it,
and then instantly imagining myself exhilarated

with its speed which becomes my own.
What I didn't want to accept is that I think about your
        full moon
eyes
all the time. That I think about sorcery. Other sailors
and cowboys. Even now, as I sit here in the old night
watching for the morning.
                        I don't want these thoughts,
as the tangled bare branches of winter lace
themselves against the past-shadowed, still dark early
        morning
sky.


## OLD JASON IN SAN JOSE

(Key, Key, What Bird Sings That Song?)


He's there, living among the computer chips
and large Vietnamese population. His name appears
on expensive speaker systems, though I doubt if it is his
        family
which owns that company. I don't know any more how one
survives blue dogs barking at the moon. I imagine
Stone Key, where they have such delicious crabs,
and think of driving the chain of keys, connected by snaking
bridges which gave me hallucinations, the bars snapping
at my eyes, trying to draw me into the water. But I am
drawn also to places where women and men are
distorted; how could I not have learned about images
in the photo-darkroom of California adolescence?

I thought I was searching for truth,
but when I found it I was so horrified
that I locked myself into this room in the Midwest
with plenty of windows, no curtains, and no key. No need
ever to go out again
into the world.
                              I disguise myself,
complaining of age, use my
old lady mask to give credence
to my life in this room. I am screened
away from the embarrassments, the
rejections and denied failures of sexual
encounter.
                         That's one side of the
story. The other is the terrible truth,
that women are neutered with age,
blue dogs barking at the moon,
—Medea's rage when Jason takes a younger woman—
and men continue their adventures;
                              he lives in San Jose with his wife
and children, probably grandchildren, and still has
everything. Constellations turn,
two lions born only hours apart, one
destiny male, one female. Is that the key? the difference
between two lives begun
in the California orange groves,
where the dusty leaves rustle against
bright gold fruit. He owned it; I ate it.
Could that difference be the subject
of so many tales?

# LION MIRROR

for David Green and other

Troubadours.
He is dark,
lion dark, and I imagine
the antelope girl
he reached for, with her tan thighs,
and her mouth of chocolate and raspberries.
On a veldt, a plain, nothing like this Midwestern
ground, near a watering hole where the gazelles
were always lifting their prong-horned heads
to the wind, he found her, no—
he stalked her there.

I don't even imagine
men like these
in love with me. Their
hands so capable of holding
Mont Blanc pens or power saws,
writing checks or building boats,
they'd hardly notice someone
like me. But would that
matter in a world where I sat
at a keyboard and pounded out Chopin
or Mozart by the hour, or even one
where my other talents might
wear a suit? I think that

this world I live in
is one that makes my
unbeautiful self more visible,
makes me wonder why I
see him as a lion,
and imagine his gazelle lust
and do not even think of myself
as other than, perhaps, a palm
tree, old and dusty resident
next to the watering hole.

The Rose Diner
Los Angeles

Dear Craig,

If I am Medea, why do I need Jason so much? It is
clear that he should need me, my magical powers, my
knowledge of the Golden Fleece, but why am I
drawn to him, to so many Jasons? Why do I fall into
their full-moon eyes, want to ski their powdery
slopes, think of them as lions, focus on them so much
when what is most beautiful to me is the orchid or
the moon. I say I don't love female images, yet that
is plainly not true. There must be     something I am
missing
    that I search for in Jason,

some beauty that could never be female because I am female.

After many years, I re-watched Cocteau's haunting film, *La Belle et la Bête* (Beauty and the Beast). I had completely forgotten that, like Medea, who has to betray her father in order to help Jason gain The Golden Fleece, Beauty has to betray her father (she asks him to bring back the forbidden rose) in pursuit of what she loves, or what seems beautiful to her. And I had forgotten the lovely fairy-tale magic which Cocteau injects into the film with the five talismans or magic tokens of the Beast's power, of which the rose is the most important. I know that when I first saw that film, I thought it was the story of my life, but now I wonder if I didn't identify as much with the Beast as with Beauty. After all, like Belle, what I wanted was to be the rose, the symbol of perfect organic beauty and love, but I saw myself, not as Belle but like the Beast, imprisoned in an ugly exterior, longing for beauty.

Yr Lady of The Garden in East Lansing

# BEAUTY AND THE BEAST

*after the Cocteau film, for Frank O'Hara*

"La Belle, La Belle," I remember him
whispering, walking the corridor lined with candles,
but I remembered it wrong, it is she who races the corridors
searching for him. I didn't remember either
that a rose caused it all, her father picking a rose to fulfill
        her request,
and then being asked to pay for it with his life. How much
        I didn't
remember about this story which I once identified with, as all
Cinderella stories have drawn me into their ashy jewel boxes.

I remember saying breathlessly, after that first viewing,
"but he was handsomer as the beast," and totally forgetting
that her boorish wastrel suitor at home is played by the same
        actor
who wears the mask and only as a beast is willing to give
        her the
key. The key is a real key
actually, a golden one,
and comes at a point in the film
when the beast says something else
I hadn't remembered: that there are five things
which are the source of his secret —
a rose, his mirror, the white horse, the key, and his

39

glove. Oh, how could anyone resist this story?
Who cares that the author himself
did not love women or was, in the modern phrase,
a substance abuser?
He lived to be old, famous, rich, and very successful.

But would anyone care about this if he had not offered
        the image
of the man as a lion, giving the golden key to his treasure
        house
to a girl who asked, as a gift from a father's journey,
only a rose and saw herself beautiful in a mirror
which showed her successful sisters as
ugly?
                I didn't want La Bete, "Ma Bete" as she runs
through the corridors calling him, to be the offish real suitor,
or a man at all. I censored the entire ending of the movie,
not remembering she as princess and he as prince,
looking cartoonish, flying off to his kingdom
like crude versions of Superman and Lois.

The movie ended for me when she holds the lion beast in
        her arms and
looks into his eyes, something he's told her never to do.
        That's what I
see as fulfillment, when she sees that he is an animal, not
        a disguised
man, an animal trying to raise himself, impossibly, to a
        human level.
*Not* that enchantment gave him bestiality but the opposite:
that enchantment
can force the beast of self
to try to dress, live, love
like a man,
                beyond his nature, and thus be

more beautiful to a woman than any
manly form could ever be.

That's what I loved about the movie
and still moves me. Women, myself, we
need to love a beast, to feel that it could transcend
itself for love, for us, for beauty. I mis-remembered him,
        the Beast,
running through
the castle, calling, "La Belle, La Belle"; instead,

it was she
running through the corridors calling,
"Ma Bete, Ma Bete," loving him because he would die
        for her.
I misremembered what actually happened, wanting him
to utter these words, "La Belle, La Belle,"
this monster who loved Beauty
so much he gave away the glove,
the mirror, the rose, his horse,
the key. The Beast is always there;
it is beauty we must search for so desperately.

The Ritter Cafe
Vienna

Dear Jonathan,

Let's see, what's new. Not much, except I have fallen
under the spell of a hot new intellectual historian/
critic named Camille Paglia. Her book *Sexual Personae*

which I've just started to read makes me feel like I am looking in a mirror at someone who has agreed with my ideas and then taken them the final distance. I am almost afraid of finishing the book, for fear of disappearing, or something like that. But she is also like a drug. I am afraid of taking too much. I am afraid her ideas would consume me. Yes, she might steal my soul. Here's a taste from


Yr Lady in East Lansing,

DW


How did beauty begin? Earth-cult, suppressing the eye, locks man in the belly of mothers. There is, I insisted, nothing beautiful in nature. Nature is primal power, coarse and turbulent. Beauty is our weapon against nature; by it we make objects, giving them limit, symmetry, proposition. Beauty halts and freezes the melting flux of nature.

Beauty was made by men acting together. Hamlets, forts, cities, spread across the Near East after the founding of Jericho (ca. 8000 B.C.), the first known settlement in the world. But it was not until Egypt that art broke its enslavement to nature. High art is non utilitarian. That is, the art object, though retaining its ritualism, is no longer a tool of something else. Beauty is the art object's license to life. The object exists on its own, godlike. Beauty is the art object's light from within. We know it by the eye. Beauty is our escape from the murky flesh-envelope that imprisons us.

Camille Paglia, Sexual Personae

---

# ORCHID BREATH

*for Camille Paglia, a meditation
on Mary Oliver's poem, "Sleeping
in the Forest"*

There is nothing earthy about me, friends.
I cannot imagine with pleasure
lying down on the forest floor, with fiddle head
ferns playing lacy scherzos when I fall asleep. I cannot
feel comfortable with the dampness which unglues
the slug from mushroom death, and the arms of the tree
      boughs
do not welcome me or soothe me. I don't feel
in touch with some earthy woman
who wears welcoming skirts of humus
in which another woman might lie down and feel
comforted by tender browns and greens.
                          I see
the flash of the blue jay,
      like steel, and hear
            the woodpecker hammering dead wood.
I ache with the moisture, the damp

rots me rather than lowering my fever.
I would find no pleasure lying there under a redwood
if a slender snake of the forest crawled expediently
over my ankle. I would in fact not want to return to any
garden which was not attached to a house, the house being
the place I would live, the garden, the woods only the place
     I might
occasionally walk,
                where I would see things so unlike me
that
I would find them beautiful.
But beauty is something I want
behind or beneath glass.
My hands would turn
into slug-fingers, sausage, meat
without the transparent glass
to separate me
from the forest realm
which would draw me down into its mulch,
to lose my orchid breath,
be crushed with dead men's fingers
to be crowned only in gesture,
my gold teeth gleaming out of my skull.

## THE ROSY CORN GODDESS

This is the year when I want to wear velvet—the velvet of
pansies, of horses' eyes, of the caps of Medieval pages—
more than I ever have, though it has always been
my favorite fabric. And in the malls
that glitter with tinsel, every shop
has dresses that flow over the model's shoulders
in the colors of midnight, of swamps and orchids,
of tarnished metals beautiful for their patinas.

What if we Americans lived in a world where men
wore tuxedos and women danced in their satin shoes
until dawn and I were one of them?
Naked and pale, like a painting on velvet,

45

I imagine the phone like a box of chocolate-covered cherries,
dark exterior, inner heart of words and red messages.
Forget the mall; the velvety red-headed black and white
woodpecker,
out on my winter-bare oak tree, is an enchanted
lover who flies outside the window.
One I can never touch.

I ask myself if my experience
looking into the expensive shop window
at the velvet dress night-flowing over the model's shoulders
is the same one I had when I was ten and saw pansies
for the first time,
how I wanted to take them inside myself,
own them,
make them part of me
—their beauty?

The feeling is the same, of course,
but what causes such feelings, makes the difference between
Michelangelo, say, and a woman who fills her house
with flashy knickknacks? Or buys a wardrobe filled with
            soft or
glittering clothes she
only wears once?

As women, perhaps we are giant ears of maize,
sweet kernelled, phallic even, not braided like wheat,
corny. Buttered ears.

Velvet is lips, all lips.
And good taste as we would insist on—art, that is,
does it indicate morality? A better person if you collect
first editions rather than two hundred pairs

of beautiful shoes, or figurines
shaped like ducks or cats?

Touching is the source of disease, contagion.

This cloth, like skin, is beautiful because it makes you
want to touch it. Touching with the eyes rather than the
          hands—
does that lead to good taste, to a good life? In this observer-
created universe is it the first act
of morality?

Like Paglia, I believe in Beauty, and I believe that it
is something we have to labor to create. I see myself
in the tradition of Courtly Love and Poetry as that
Cavalier art in which we carry on some of the
greatest accomplishments of civilization. In my
lifetime quest for beauty, I have searched for both the
perfect lover and attempted to create the ideal self.
You are my most loyal courtier, Craig, the first of a
line of Troubadours who have shown up at poetry
readings and later in classrooms, all questing for
Creeley's, mine, Stevens' rose of language. The perfect
words, the poems, of love and beauty.


Yr orchid lady,

DW

# PANSIES

They are faces.
As roses are hands.
They are speakers, and in the cool
mornings though reticent, a look
at one burnished
purple face
with its eyelet of yellow in the center makes me
lean closer. There is nothing to hear, I know
that.
     I don't really sentimentalize flowers.
But the act of leaning into
the pansy, the act of standing in August next to a sunflower,
taller than I, with its head bending down as if towards me,
my own hand which hovers near the glove of the rose petal
     or my peering
down into the earth to see if there's some seed cracking it
     yet — those
acts are their own kind of language. Signal my understanding
     that
there is more than the human in this civilization. If it takes
     the human
to perceive that, to understand it, then surely we must
     accept
that human state as a gift. Time to moderate our wisdom
     "Better to give than receive."
Easier, maybe, but so incomplete.

I am listening to the pansies this morning,
and though I hear nothing,
it is not
because there is
nothing there
to hear.

## HIS BEDROOM VOICE

He leaves a message on our answering machine,
a simple one, plain, expedient, he needs a
letter of recommendation, but as I listen without
much thought/I realize I don't mind anything he asks of me;
in fact I like this young man,
find it easy to be interested in whatever he does, and the
        voice
comes on the tape which unrolls,
        no longer telling the story of my life,
like
the petals of a rose opening up,
not a radio voice or a singer's voice,
just a human voice; why do I think of it as petals?
There is a folding quality to it, turning, rolling, inward,
it is the voice of a lover
lying in bed saying something simple, plain, something
        expedient like
"I wish I didn't have to get up just now."

Isn't this interesting, I think/this voice, does it sound this
        way
to a man? Or do I hear it like this because I am a woman?
The other young troubadours don't like him very much;
Geoffrey says he wears garage mechanic shirts, as if somehow
        his
hands
are too greasy for poetry. "He doesn't care about poetry,"
        they say,
"just wants to BE a poet." It embarrasses them, who have
        all had
quiet passionate and blighted love affairs which they NEVER
        talk
about explicitly, that he
so publicly fell in love this summer and told everyone. I
        suppose
that appealed to me, but now I hear this Jason's voice,
which is not talking to me
particularly, just as a rose I cut
from the bush in the garden has not
bloomed its blushing self for me, but I regard it as my own
personal beautiful artifact on that day when I put it in a
        glass
next to my desk.
I've always heard a voice speaking to me
while making love.
It too was my rose/maybe this is all there is:
the voice, unrolling on
the tape,
the message trivial,
so much more significant
    in timbre
        than diction or content.

50

# THE COFFEE BRUSH

We sniffed it,
they said. What a
fragrance.

I smiled, thinking
of those handsome young men
holding the small paintbrush that I use
to sweep out my coffee grinder
after it has pulverized my Chocolate Raspberry Coffee Beans,
holding the brush to their regal
poetry-writing noses
in our kitchen
while Steel Man and I are eating
thin-crusted pizza in Chicago
and they are kindly taking in our mail
and browsing in our winter absence.

# RED SILK SCARF

Wearing his long coat
he walks into the room.
I expect that he will be carrying a skateboard,
but he is not. I know that this magician
must have in his pocket silk scarves
which with long fingers he will pull and pull
out and out. No silliness like white
rabbits, or the accoutrements of aristocracy —
black top hat, morning coat or tails.
I know he wouldn't be cruel enough to carry
snakes in his pockets, but I know that he
controls me with his hands which know how to touch
lightly
anything,
    a stone, and a drop of water will appear,
    my desk, and a small green frog will be sitting there
    the cardinal red scarf, which he draws out of his pocket
        and
        convinces me it must have my name on it.

There is nothing I can say,
though my lips ought to be able
to ask him why
he doesn't love women
so well as men. I could never ask this question

of any man, which is why I write it down and write
      it down
with my red inked pen,
as if I am being punished for a schoolgirl failure.

You have to look far back into the past
to find women as sorcerers, and even then
they've often been rewritten into false beauty,
their snaky heads covered and disguised,
their talon hands sheathed with silk and jewels.

This young man walks by me like Christian Slater in his
      long wool
coat
and engaging smile. I smile back.
Maybe he already knows we are both
magicians? Maybe he doesn't,
but that is what I am here

to teach him.

# ICE

*for Craig Hamilton in response to
his poem "The Stench"*

It is the machines we strap on to our bodies
which distinguish us
from animals.
The skate
     whose silver blade is like
     someone wiping tears
     off your face,
     then slapping you
     for crying
screes, whooshes, slurps
flying particles of frozen watery chemical
in a noisy cloud against the bent foot.
Figure eights are the sign of
infinity, moving the body into a
T'ai Chi of unblocked energy.

The ski
     like a long wooden pencil
     writing slalom poems
     or a baroque-patterned fork bringing
     out-of-season vegetables up to
     your lips
comets, parallels, orbits

huge slopes of space,
some marked with flags which
the body curves in toward or away from,
a proprioception of breath.

In my coffee cup, round as a crystal ball, I don't see
an Olympic-sized swimming pool, green with chlorination,
and marked with black-strip racing lanes. Instead, I
see the bog, the marsh this ice might
melt into, the stool-colored muddy place
where humans are invisible
and grope for survival.

Out in the icy, silver-medalled world
we demonstrate how different we
are from other forms of life
by strapping machines to our bodies
and dancing as elaborately as single molecules,
while in the coffee cup there is only chaos,
motion which leads to random results,
no gold or silver
medal racing, no beauty,
no poems or elegant meals with asparagus forks,
nothing but death,
and that without glory,
an avalanche of either mud or snow,
which no human eye witnesses.

The Ritter Cafe
Vienna


Dear Jonathan,

You are the novelist, the story teller, but even you
resort to magic as a most satisfactory source of action
and resolution. I remain obsessed with "realistic"
magic, that attractive theory from quantum physics
which allows the possibility of many parallel universes
where each moment could project an infinite number
of alternative narratives. Well, perhaps not an infinite
number, but more than one story becomes possible.
Was there only one Jason, one Medea? One sorceress?
One sailor?

---

Quantum Reality #4: The many-worlds interpretation (Reali-
ty consists of a steadily increasing number of parallel universes.)
. . . Invented in 1957 by Hugh Everett, a Princeton graduate
student, the many-worlds interpretation is a latecomer to the
New Physics scene . . . Everett's proposal is particularly attrac-
tive to theorists because it resolves, as we shall see, the major
unsolved puzzle in quantum theory—the notorious quantum
measurement problem. . . .

Everett saw it like this: the orthodox ontology treats measure-
ment as a special kind of interaction, yet we know that

*measurement interactions cannot really be special* since M devices are no different from anything else in the world. How, then asks Everett, can we strip the measurement act of its privileged status and achieve within physics that *democracy of interactions* which certainly prevails in nature?

* * *

Everett represents everything by proxy waves, but he leaves out the wave function collapse. When a quantum system encounters an M device set to measure a particular attribute, it splits as usual into many waveforms, each corresponding to a possible value of that attribute. What is new in Everett's model is that correlated to every one of these system wave functions is a different M-device waveform which records one of these attribute values. Thus if the measure attribute has five possible values, the quantum-entity-plus-measuring-device develops into five quantum systems, each with a different attribute value paired with five measuring devices each registering that value. Instead of collapsing from five possibilities to one actual outcome, the quantum system in Everett's interpretation realizes *all five outcomes.*

Nick Herbert, *Quantum Reality: Beyond the New Physics*

Jonathan, I seem to have chosen to live in the plainest
universe. After all that gambling with my life, I
choose now to live in this safe Garden of the Midwest
traveling to Las Vegas twice a year, where my only
risk is the inevitable one of aging or playing games
where I don't win money.

It's the young Troubadours who keep reminding me
of all those other (perhaps parallel) stories, lives.

Yr Lady of the Mirrors,

DW

## HOUSE OF CARDS

*For Geoffrey, Chris, Christian,*
*Richard and Brad*

The tall guy who wears the cowboy hat
and whose jeans are always ripped enough to make you
aware of his skin, the one whose eyes
are like pansies, the macho guy who says
he's not very smart, but that he loves poetry —
walking down the hall in front of me as I head for the
        LADIES,
he for the snack machine where he always gets a pint of
        milk, tall.

58

I find I love to talk to him, fall into those eyes
as if they are jeweler's boxes which could hold enough poems
to change civilization, if poetry
changed anything. His eyes are so different
from the dark bicycle rider with grey eyes, who looks
and looks, without ever blinking, reads in a monotone, stares
as if at destiny and is simply filled to the roots of himself
with the desire to be heard. There are so many of them
                    who gather
in
that room with me, as we worship the elegance of an idea
or a turn of phrase.

The young man who wears the long tweed coat
and writes sonnets better than mine ever were, who laughs
                    with
his eyes, and the thin one
who boldly says that he'd like
to be Lord Byron while in fact
holding behind his quiet almost frozen eyes
nothing but icy pure
intelligence. Opposites. The attraction, I suppose. A young
father, who writes about ice fishing and male bonding
whose eyes are ears and must have been turned
in the womb towards Orpheus' lyre
as he ascended from the watery dark,

I, who gave up motherhood,
some Thursdays when I see these young men,
am filled with a strange sense of family pride. Imagined sons
and lovers. No, what a bunch of kings and jacks! What
          a hand!
What aces they are.
Some rewards come late and are so diffuse
no one but the winner knows there has been a stake
          gambled.

I think of that
on Thursday afternoons, as I pick up my cards,
never less than a Full House.
And often, as I have never had in poker,

a Royal Flush.

## WHITE SHIRT IN THE CLASSROOM

She depicts white shirts hanging in her bathroom,
their arms touching her wet lingerie, and I send her to
Wilbur — "Love Calls Us to Things of This World." Steel
     Man
shops for a black shirt which can be worn, buttoned to
     the collar
and without a necktie, to formal
occasions, and buys a white one because he looks so
     clean-cut/
the black one makes him
disappear. I notice that Kevin Costner
wears a white one buttoned up, no tie, when all the other
     men are in
tuxedoes and he's drinking champagne in the Jim Harrison
     movie
and yesterday, there he was, the young
magician, the one who
wears the long tweed coat,
his hair in wings like Scott Fitzgerald
gleaming in the classroom with his white shirt,
buttoned at the throat, appropriately baggy,

60

and without a tie,
and I find myself in front of the class talking
about the cliché that women are sexier with clothes on
than off, and in order not to be a sexist, I find myself saying
and men, of course, too, as I look at the white shirt
            buttoned to the
chin
and wonder if I'd like him better with a tie and secretly
            relieved
that I would never have to see him
no matter how handsome
nude of clothing, naked physically,
or stripped to his most private parts,
the elegant words which like black tie
keep us safely flirting and away,
away safely,
reassuringly, happily, away
completely away from sex, love or romance.

## POLITESSE

We can't even say his name any more
            Galahad
without simpering images of a dandy.
But he was the one, along with Percival,
      whose name has gotten even worse associations—
            nerds with their hair parted in the middle,
            glasses and braces, the dumb brain—
the one to accomplish the quest for the Grail.

*  *  *

Yes, I like these boys who are so polite,
who call me Professor or Ma'am.

Some are tall, with torn jeans and cowboy hats,
others with wingtip shoes, tweed coats and Irish hair.
Some have Spanish surnames though they don't speak a word
of good Spanish, and others write with Mont Blanc pens
or drive sports cars very fast. But they all
love women, gaze at the silver ankle, kiss it,
touch lily hands, dewdrop lips,
and whisper in the ears of all women
their respect, "politesse," I'd like
to call it. They're troubadours
who remind us of the complicated
stories inscribed in our DNA:

    spring and all the attendant petals,
    May wine, with wild strawberries,
    cupping the words of chivalry,
    to their lips, exchanging
the molecules of polite address.

# THE TALL BOY

Beach sand makes you aware
that glass is spun out of its grainy voice,
by the men with big lungs

and chests like overnight cases carried
            on to the train,
pushing air through rock.
That there is an array of sand under
your white body
            which smells like coconut cookies,
and the glassblower's breath is getting hotter
as it soughs up through the sand, transforming it,
turning the day to glass. The Pacific out there—
a lover who has rejected you.

Diet Pepsi's still cold,
            as you remember him to be towards the end.
The chilled bottle's better than Dom Perignon.
And your sandwich of thick cheese and lettuce and mustard
on French bread is a marriage of cottonsoft and crust.
Even the Dijon wants to touch your lips.
            No rejections.
            A good lunch never
            never does that.
There is an Asian Pear Apple
also, its texture like ice cubes, its taste of melon,
            the black seeds
            which could be the pupils
            of his eyes, though not so round, no—more
            like those diamond-shaped pupils
            you see on the lynx/the seeds
            slightly tangy, almost sour, alongside
            the meat of the Pear.
Voice and eye on this June day.
I want to believe that I could still
sit on a glassy beach.
Eat a picnic,
            a straw mat under my old-lady legs,
                as white as new

cotton underwear
or coconut,
listen to the breathing,
    as if I were lying next to him after we had made love,
and I want to believe that there would be
    no rejection,
that there would be love
    expanding, blowing into my body,
the food
    would be shared and salty
        with more than mustard. I,
poised, next to his motionless body,
    not touching. Unwilling
to disturb the sleeper.

## WHY HE LOVES JOHN LENNON

Secrets are in his head
like sugar cubes in a white porcelain bowl.
The lid lifted, autumn afternoon pours in.
Not a string quartet, not Beethoven, but
Penny Lane is in yr ears, the cadences of someone who
        collects
coins, page after page of wheat ear pennies
which won't buy anything, not
life or death.
He loves John Lennon because Lennon is sugar;

he died and spilled chocolate blood, his
songs came out of a mind full of secrets, Scorpion rich,
and he never drank tea.

He tells me I will die from it. Too much tea.
Or from too many glasses of red wine, rich as blood.
He knows I don't really care about sugar, my
triglyceride reading probably beats his cholesterol level
        which is
very low,
in low levels/what does any of this matter
if someone shoots you and before you even reach the
        ambulance
you are dead?

I saw yellow autumn leaves fall like coins,
through the mountain air, at a roadside park where
the boy and I were stopped for lunch. Eating our
apples and cheese, drinking pure water,
I turned and for a moment saw the coins swirling
in a circle of air.

I love this young man, as if he were a son.
But I don't understand him very well. I accept his
love for John Lennon, as I would accept his love
for his father, a husband I might be estranged or divorced
        from,
but what he loves most remains locked in his head,
as we drive for hours and miles along the West Coast of
        the World,

and listen to the music which generated so much money
for so many people, and this boy dreams of his grandfather
the banker, and his father who made money
but died young,

and I return home to pour a cup of tea
which I drink plain,
without cream, milk,
certainly without sugar. How many lumps?

None, thank you. The tea is amber,
clear, the color of a penny.

---

The Rose Diner

Dear Craig,

When I moved to New York from California in
1960, I took the desert with me, along with my
hunger for civilization and particularly my desire for
the man-made world of big buildings, museums,
libraries and restaurants where chefs prepared the
food. Yet, it was being in New York which made me
define myself as a Californian. For the first time I felt
the power of being a Westerner, and I loved the aura
of sunshine which just mentioning Southern California
seemed to radiate. I fiercely became a California Girl.
I don't think I ever had a tan when I grew up in
Southern California, but the minute I became a New
Yorker and rode the train every weekend to Reis Park
where I toasted myself as brown as a 9 to 6, six-day-
a-week bookstore clerk could get in New York City.

I have never understood, though many have offered
interpretations, why so many men attracted to me

throughout my life have been gay men. I wonder sometimes if it is that nun-like demeanor I seem to have? Something pure or white or untouchable about the way I look, I guess. Whatever it was that made the blackjack dealer in Las Vegas ask me if I were a nun; and maybe it draws men who have no use for actual earthy or sexual women in their lives. The good side of this is that it has made it possible for me to form real friendships with men, since sex does not become a distraction. But it has also given me the same life as an adult that I had as a child, one which seems to be lived devoid of the sensuous. No wonder I over-value food, adulate the body, seek the macho, and have so over-valued sex.

It should prepare me to be old, I guess, since people truly don't see women over fifty as sexual images. Yet, perhaps I cling to youth, shun aging precisely because I feel I still have not yet been perceived as the sexual woman I have always felt myself to be.


Yr Lady of the California Coast,

DW

# THE PONY EXPRESS RIDER

*for George Stanley*

It was so hot in that apartment/Harold
and Dora cooking out of Elizabeth David in spite
of the sauna effect of New York's lower east side
tenement apartment/ I, only invited because
of my friendship with you/so confusing;
you riding the old nag of Jack Spicer poetics
and I running behind, holding a letter
I'd forgotten to post, your mailbag full
of the Maximus letters, another mailbag in
Brooklyn full of bedtime stories featuring animals.
What did we eat that day, me fussing as if I had on
white gloves, still wearing my patent leather shoes
with grosgrain bows, under the full-skirted summer
seersucker dress. You laughed at me, but found
me alluring, just as if I were Alice or some other forbidden
little Victorian girl. I hadn't yet put on my Dale Evans
boots, or changed the skirt for cowboy jeans; hadn't yet
become a rider myself, or understood why I needed
mail so much, why I'd go to any length to meet each Pony
Express Rider, overwhelmed and anxious for any letter
which might be addressed to me.

This is not a story, only an image.
Wandering in the house, as I did in my dream again
last night, finding another closet, this one with a coat made

up of hundreds of old dresses sewn together elegantly.
The "coat" first worn by the dog in the dream, then
the dog transformed into me wearing the coat-dress.

I am never a rider in this
dream, only a wanderer, through some house which goes on
and on, is infinite, and composed of many different living
warrens, some shabby and poor, like that sweltering
        apartment
where you took me for our Provencal lunch. In the dream
I am always lost, always. All the addresses of my life
scrapbooked together into this infinite dwelling
where I never know what name or number will be
affixed to the outside door, where I could never
receive mail, where no Pony Express Rider could ever
        find me,
but then why is that any different from my life? Dreams
only tell us what we already know.

---

The Rose Diner

Craig,

I had a dream in which there was a closet with a black
coat. It was connected with the fact that when I first
moved to New York City from California I didn't own
a winter coat. Or boots, for that matter. It wasn't until

69

my second year in New York that I could afford a coat, and I vividly remember the pleasure of buying this heavy black wool coat at Macy's. I don't know how that got tied up in my dream with Marjorie Perloff, the critic whose praise I have longed for all these years. Many strange transformations in this dream. You in it too.

## SNOW HANDS

He's pale,
rosebud lips,
the face of an altar boy,
pretends to smoke a cigarette
when he's with Steel Man,
whose Marlboros are a reminder
of bad boys cutting class to smoke
and talk dirty/but he plays blackjack
like an old timer, poker-faced,
white fingers ready to pull hundred dollar bills
from his wallet, always doubling his losing hands

can't leave the table where his money is.

I dream of a closet where I cannot find the winter
coat, black, heavy,

woolen cage for my white
body, bought against snow when I was
young and fresh from Southern
California.

I never hid inside clothing
when I lived in Orange County. But this boy
grew up encased in snow boots, heavy parkas,
thick gloved against North Eastern Winters. Now he plays
        blackjack
without guile, uncoated, wanting only a Southern California
        tan
to shield him, protect him from Bad Luck.

Old Coyote, Shadow Self, Wind Breath
deals snow hands. Hundred dollar bills turn white too
like zeros of snow, disappear, vanish/why,
he thinks, is there snow
on the desert? In the dream
I never find the coat,
only an expensive version of it
which belongs to somebody else. Today, he's being
dealt Roses and Snow Queens, and cannot win
a hand. He needs gloves, a magic glove, to cover
these hands of snow. Once he turns this into Winter's game
he'll know how to win again. And I will
search and search for the heavy black coat, lost
in the infinite closet of myself.

This dream had a great deal to do with my desire to be accepted and loved. My sense that men are so remote that they could never love me, and the equal sense that women are threatening, witch-like in their power. Perhaps that's why Perloff was in the dream, representing the androgynous power of the critic whose love is so mysterious, remote, threatening and hard to win.

Yr Lady of Dreamlight,

DW

# DOGS

(A Meditation on Gertrude Stein in an
Armchair Sitting Under Picasso's
Portrait of Her in Paris)

*for Barbara, Wendy & Judith*

Like a children's book illustrator's large
                              dog,
                                        wearing a dress,

her wedge-shaped head above
                    these human accoutrements,
                                        she sits upright
and ready to talk human speech.

What story
are you telling? I ask. She has
never looked at me, though she looks
seriously at the children who listen to her tales,
and to the other animals which gather around when she
is speaking of rabbits and little pigs.

The border collies who almost eternally hold
a green with moss tennis ball in their teeth, waiting for
        a human
to throw it, again and again, work the sheep as their wool,
five bags full, gets spongy with mist and the bush of it puffs
into walking pillows. Outside, the window or door, they
        stand,
holding the
ball, eyes trained on any human hands they can see
through the pane. But Hags, poetfriends, old women smile
in the distance, their children grown. And the dogs know
        they are
the ones who will be walking with them. Their gods,
border collies or black labs, are now the only ones who
        will walk
with them, on the beach, in the woods,
through vine covered hills or
the moss hung live oaks.

Dog Ladies,
we all of us are, though my dog is only
a ghost, the thin Doberman snarling in a Manhattan
        apartment

73

or outside as I walked her on rainy broken streets,
she pulling the leash to create a strong leather line between
        hand
and
throat, my white face next to her black one, a sheepskin
        around my
shoulders. This painted portrait of me, John Singer Sargent's
*Madame X,*
with a black dress, and now we have added a black dog,
hangs over my life to remind me that behind the ground
of the painting was a bedroom, with a closed door, where the
motorcycle
betrayer lay in bed, smoking, reading Dr. Williams poems
and dreaming of raising sheep in Vermont, building a house,
in which he could live like Thoreau, without women,
        without trouble,
in civil disobedience and singular joy.


He is there now, and I am not Madame X but the dog lady
of Picasso's painting. This is my story, young men and
        women,
you who listen to me: Once upon a time there was a white
        rabbit
named
Jason, and he popped up like a white fluffy sheep, out of a
        silk hat,
black as Judith's Labrador retriever, Pearl. Jason loved the
        moon
and its whiteness, but he had a problem, he needed the
        fleece,
the magic fleece of a sheep that only a woman could touch.


No, this is not my story, but it is the story
I know how to tell. I see you waiting for more,
but you must look at these paintings, and then the photos of

74

these women who walk with their dogs,
                        who when there is mist of fog
or rain softly swirling around them, must think they are one
of the Brontë sisters, seeing out from Haworth, onto
the moors, and while we all know some stories
have better endings than others, what none of us wants
        to admit
is that the end of one story is/must be
the beginning of another.

For the color, we need a bird,
a flashing cardinal, cobalt tinted blue jay,
the flash of magpie black and white,
to fly quickly in and out of
the picture. Dog Ladies, Sheep Men,
children or old men and women
listening to stories.

## WHEN CANNED PEACHES
## TURN INTO MAPLELIGHT

It glows
the small yellow maple
behind the picket fence in grey
autumn damp.
It's like a bowl of commercially canned
peaches, smooth, shiny globes from being skinned,
cut by machine, loaded with
sugar syrup which makes them shine
like greasepaint under klieg lights.

For years they've both been there,
the tree and the image:
one moment which has no meaning to me
except as an emblem of pain, defeat,
impossible failure.
Sitting at the metal kitchen dinette table
in Southern California of the fifties,
blue cardiganned elbows
resting on metal, the bowl with the one
glistening peach half in its clear syrup in front of me,
a dime store spoon, blue and white kitchen
curtains, late afternoon in California's
linoleum autumn, feeling sorry for myself,
knowing I was trapped, a pregnant girl
with no husband, one who knew how lonely
a child is without a father, one who knew how
terrible the poverty of white-collared working mothers
        could be,
one who hated women with no life but children and earning
        a bare
living,
one who did not want a child who would hate her
for all the things she hated her own mother for,
one who wanted to define herself differently
and now was trapped, eating an unhealthy, unattractive
commercially canned peach, an image of her mother's life
where you played bad music by ear and only watched
        Hollywood
musicals because the good movies were about problems;
and who could possibly want, she said, to watch other
        people
suffering?

Like several hundred garish, unreal-looking
canned peach halves, the leaves on my Michigan
backyard maple wave at me.
They have turned into a beauty
I never expected, one I longed for but never
hoped I would actually achieve.
How can I reject old age, then,
or death if it is all part of this transformation?
                                        Because
I am still the girl sitting at the white metal table
crying into sugar, eating sunshine
in whatever form I can get it?

## MAPLELIGHT

*For Craig Cotter, who might be my son*

He could recite the random number list
backward. He caught a big fish,
a Cutthroat Trout, a Whitefish? a Muskellunge,
something you'd photograph/he looked like someone
else.

Yellow leaves, no gold,
almost as dark as the flesh of
an acorn squash, are flying out of the small Maple
in my Michigan backyard. This place is beautiful if
you have the eyes for it.

My eyes still settle more comfortably
on palm trees, or brown rolling hills, desert
scenes with Yucca bells and Joshua Trees
and yearn for camellia bushes with so many
long lasting flowers they'd turn brown on the bush,
waxy leaves, related to Magnolias;
Southern California is not the South.

He lives in California where Hummingbirds
are common. Near a haunted canyon where
accidents always occur when he walks.
He's spent his life putting soft
and hard together, the numbers
like stone, mineral truth, unflinching,
and the sport fish transformed into electric blue,
lemon yellow, striped angels, trigger fish,
of aquarium beauty, always undulating, soft-fleshed,
changing from minute to minute.

He could recite the random number list
backward. He caught a big fish,
a Cutthroat Trout, a Whitefish? a Muskellunge,
something you'd photograph/he looked like someone
else. Just my Michigan eyes, I guess, converted
from Southern California eyes shaded with dark lenses.

I see Maples in autumn, not
as syrup,
or as my husband does, like leaves to be raked,
but as light. Lighted hands,
waving at me from the back yard.
The light of the desert,
the light of autumn, the light

before I pack my bags
and return to some other place/

yes, yes, this morning bathed
in Maplelight!

---

## CELLOPHANE BURN

In the orange grove where I watched spiders
whose fat coin bodies seemed so much more precious
than silver dimes, the hummers came spinning
through, looking for flowers with deep throated
flagons, or like children, for red sugar juice to suck.

Anna's Hummingbird, or Costa's. No matter: I called all
     I saw
"Ruby Throated." They flashed their brooches
of red so that I wanted my own throat to buckle with
iridescent voice. But my Sunday blue velvet jumper
with red satin blouse never gave me the quickness of light,
nor the cellophane burn of those fast wings, those
motor spins fueled by liquid sugar.
I believe we think falsely of the hummingbird as silent
or without a voicing call, with only the sound of the wings
to be heard as it spins. My voice was a silver dime,
and it could be spent on a red Popsicle or milk at school.
My black high-topped shoes and yellow hair ribbons made
     me a bee,

or one of the black and yellow spiders I watched in the
       groves.
Spin, spin, make a pattern, make a table, a web to hold
       your design.
Buzz, buzz, gather syrup, flower sap, store it for your
       queen.
This is how the world saw you, saw me, the bee girl, the
spider child when the hummingbird dazzled itself down into
the cool orange grove, catching the glint of a little silver
       dime
replacing or changing sound into light.

## HUMMINGBIRDS, DAZZLING IN FROM THE CALIF. DESERT

*for Craig Cotter and WCW*

And the apple, like a Ruby Throat, was there,
so tempting, round and perfect as
the number zero, one of those slightly
tart, sweet-taffeta flavored beauties
from New Zealand which crack against
your tongue, a fountain of glittering
snapshots.

Hummingbirds, dazzling in from the California desert,
mimic the quick motions that drive you:

playing basketball, one on one, the fast dunk of your
        thoughts
about religion and sex, about chocolate words and Beatles'
        lyrics.
But you and I disagree on what men
owe women, on the possibilities of either
sex or celibacy.
I want the longed-for
to be fulfilled
but more, I want it to be sustained. All the troubadours
I admire so much, including you—
I want them to love me more than any
other woman, but not to try to come
too close. I want to be touched with language,
and the something even more insidious—the mind
which keeps its contents secret, celibate, untouched and pure.

                    Who eats the apple
is looking for a way not to have to consume it, just as
what rises from the dead is still living. These are paradoxes,
which means they are truths. The
way I know that love cannot exist without sexual touch,
yet it does. The way I know that romantic
silliness in movies, novels, and our teenage lives
is everything and nothing; it is not love
but makes love possible. Love, invisible,
or is it just quick?—the way the hummingbird
is all quick airy motion—is nothing.

Love, love, why invent this word
if it is all zeros?

# THE BLUE JAY AT
# THE NEARLY EMPTY FEEDER

*for Jason Appelman*

There is a boy who is a blue jay of a boy,
eating apples on the shores of Lake Michigan,
the cherries of this state's Leelanau Peninsula dangling
over his head, ignored. He belongs to me
in image, but like a snake he will not be held,
wriggling in sensuous imperfection down past my wrist
dropping to the ground and disappearing into the green
        landscape.
Short dark hair, his blue chambray shirt and solid black shoes
carrying a form down the street after his revelation of failure.
He could be the actor Tom Cruise, as the cocky jet pilot,
his eyes fringed with speed, then iced by not being able to
        save the life
of his best friend. Byron, swimming the Hellespont, he too
like this boy living in extravagance, searching for poetry,
        words which
burn off his lips, kissing Sappho's foot, she just a girl who
        could never be
Orpheus, yet would not desire Eurydice's role.

No pomegranate's ever
tempted her, blood red fruit.

Poppies, yes, their scarlet cheeks/
are we talking about cherries now?
No, apples, other crimson fruit?

Old Jaybird leaves the feeder to the sparrows and finches.
I've always liked the grey breast he presents to the world,
smooth, feather-fattened, and marked by his species.
He's had his fill, and
this only a small town view,
the boy with Hades' eyes
gone to his summer at the shore.
Beyond the thicket of oaks
in my backyard, past the feeder frequented by the Jay,
receding into the distance my Pacific Ocean,
which would drown me
just like Byron if I ever dared to seek such freedom,
having found the beauty of this Midwest prison
all the beauty I can bear.

# SALT MARSH

(A Tribute to Bob Peters)

His knobbed walking stick
makes him feel like a character
in the play of his life. Sandaled feet
with bent-double toes still showing at nearly seventy
the distorting effect of ill-fitted childhood shoes.

Himself, like an Eagle with hooked beak
and predatory eyes. How he
scans the world
trying to understand
beauty which always escapes,
seeps through his fingers,
the sieve which will naturally not hold water
that is his life.

There are men with none of his power,
whose eyes have none of his forging, tooled accuracy,
who have suffered as much and come through as well
who love beauty and grace,
wake up to find it draped casually
at their elbows. Even in this outdoor sanctuary
where the whir of birds is almost orchestrated, he finds
a path which seems awkward, and we other walkers
incline and bend gracefully on spiraling paths, losing sight of
        the tall
hawk or shepherd walker's purposeful striding, knowing
        our ways
will eventually meet up. The day is crisp and salty
with good talk, but when he reappears, he is
testy and has been obviously fearful of losing us, irritated
that we did not follow his striding.

What gives some, even, poor tempered men
the power of simple line and easy beauty
when this hawk-eyed man has none
of the grace of his kind?
Why do I choose such ungainly ones
for friendship when my path is never theirs?
Why do I love these American Eagles so fiercely?

Is it that I am always interested in

the circuitous route? Knowing
otherness—might prepare me
finally to die? Why
can't I accept this simple
fact? What does the Eagle see
which I might know? Who am I: the
Snowy Egret, the Mourning Dove,

a little Burrowing Owl?

---

## CARLA BOUCHER EATS POPPIES IN SANTA FE

---

(Another Tribute to the Spirit)

We are driving the highway as straight as my Polish hair,
and Beethoven sometimes talks to us, though more often he
talks to John Lennon, and a woman you have never met is
bleaching the bones of a maverick she's found beyond the
butte, past the gorge, where the rocks change color.

One moment and the landscape is Chopined with datura
blossoms, and then there is nothing, nothing until a line
of cottonwoods crookedly marks underground green, water/
and then nothing again, for a long time, and then there is
the scattered planting of adobe buildings which lie on the
outskirts of Santa Fe.

85

With a French name, she still acts like a Polish joke: how
many Carla Bouchers does it take to screw in a light bulb?
Answer: Only one because she is the only one who knows
how. And what about the white trumpets of jimsonweed
which knock the scrub cattle out of their minds, and
            lovingly cover
arroyo banks with bloom, winding around her doorstep?

She has all these years, invaded my mind, crept into it like
a flower you wouldn't put in the salad. She is the cotton
floating through the air, of late spring cottonwoods, and her
Mayan face could be Chacmool. To men, she is The Medusa,
but to me she has been a terrible and beautiful image of
survival. She reminds me of what a maimed planet we live
on, and Jeffers' vision of the human race gone astray. I
expect to see her remove her small shoes and to have the
delicate hooves of a desert antelope. Gracefully, she should
be running away from this world and its predators, but she
opens her mouth, and the shrieking rackety voice of the blue
jay, driving all the other birds from the feeder comes out.

She's chosen the desert for growing old, and she, like a piece
of driftwood, ages well. Perhaps the hooves will dry, become
brittle, break off, and leave her stationary. Perhaps in the
spaciousness, she will need less to shriek or speak, and her
beaked mouth will crack and fall back into a soft cliff,
            a plane
of face. When a woman ages like this, no one sees her
shrill ugly youth, only the tough, gnarled clean lines of the
old wood, the twist of the returning datura vine, the
            bleached
skull, and eyes emptied of malice. May the world some day
see me also, emptied of all but this bony poetry.

# THE EMERALD TATOOED ON MY ARM

Tattoos are taboo
in the bourgeois white world.
Death camp numbers, sailors' lewd mementos of
imaginary sex, circus performers, and now the Rich Outlaws
    of heavy
metal: those Guns n' Roses guys,
marking themselves out as different. White, but
not White Bread. Mine, I cut
with a razor blade into
my arm, the letter "M" to show a
callous man how his name was sculpted
into my life.
I was only thinking of his name, "Morris," but
then my whole life was focused, in retrospect, on
so many other "M"s:
        marriage
        money
and the story of Medea, who loses
the Man
she loves.
The black bird,
flying off your arm, Jason,
in a splatter of ink
is nothing like the diving green
Mexican bird which bombed into

the windshield of the rented car
in the Yucatan, as my friends and I drove to Chichen Itza.

Nothing on that trip
made me understand
the savage world I fear: Chacmool just seemed
like a debonair man loafing on his back.
My greatest and most
dangerous adventure was in a hotel room
when I was sure, as my window rattled with Hitchcockian
menace, that I was about to be ravaged, but on
opening the shutter, I found only
a moth, huge as a baseball mitt, trapped there
and battering its fragile wings for release.

The black
bird on your shoulder, Jason,
like the M (rald) on my arm
is to remind you
of wings which brush
your face, flying away.
Keep the night
black and tattooed.
Like love
is a tattoo,
always a little taboo
on a white arm.

# THE SCULPTOR

Dear George Washington—no,
Dear Robert Morris,

Sometimes I think I made up the fact
that you had a studio in an old warehouse building
down by the Fulton Fish Market, and that I saw next door
in Marisol's studio, the wooden General George, or talked
in the hall to Mark Di Suvero,
the sculptor who was at Berkeley
during the same years
I was, whose spine was crushed in
a freight elevator transporting huge timbers
for his work. But I know I didn't make up
that first letter I wrote to you, pretending you were The
        Father of
My Country, while I was sitting in an old damp building,
and it was in Lower Manhattan,
where I could see the Brooklyn Bridge
and think of men like Hart Crane or Frank O'Hara.
They loved this city too much/ and how I did too.

Living there was what
really made me know that we were all working out
the old history of our country,
not just the new.
I didn't even know then

that you had a real name
out of Revolutionary history,
and besides I did fall in love
with George who was
our awkward ungainly president, and
thought that maybe if I transformed you into him,
out of your own smooth ambitious
smart identity, I could make you see me
as the country itself,
first growth timbered
and unexplored, Western territory
of rivers and mountains, and yes deserts
and finally an Ocean
which was all me.
                      All I wanted was you.
But, George, you were not even remotely
interested in my Western voice
once you got your commission in the army.
The dancing girls captured you, as they always
entrance the soldiers, for a while,
and then the ladies of Madison Avenue
and finally Washington, D.C. Your portrait in
the National Gallery—not quite. And you in the Corcoran
right now, on this your birthday, on the edge of the
        millennium.

George, you never made me
your First Lady. Instead, I became the
Lady in the Garden, sitting tranquilly here in the Midwest,
where our air is clean and water still plentiful,
dreaming of the Pacific Ocean which fills my mouth
        sometimes,
salty and almost human. I don't think I was mistaken
about that old woody studio, but I might have invented the
George Washington sitting on his wooden horse next door.

You were not George. You were always the other one,
whose name you bear. Though he financed the American
Revolution, we hardly remember him, and for all his wisdom
his destiny was to die in bankruptcy. He should have
        speculated more
in Western land, not taken on so much of the burden of the
        new country.

The saying is wrong. History doesn't "repeat itself," though
all things come round again, in some form or other, but
        usually not
as mirror images. I've married another "Robert," who also
has an English surname, but he loves me and is not distracted
by dancing girls or other famous ladies. Because he is
so satisfactory, I have not renamed him,
George, or anything else. But I, and all his friends call him
"Steel Man," for trustworthy strength,
as well as his muscles. It is seldom,
in fact, that I write to George Washington any more,
but today is his birthday, the bird feeder in our garden
is deserted/snow beginning to blow and swirl around the
        juniper and
spruce. And I just wanted to acknowledge a little
personal American history.

## THE SLAP

I want to tell you,
now that I've had
the dream,

91

that I understand
a little better
why you walked away from me,
why you wouldn't speak to me,
why you sneered at everything I did, even though I was
sure
that you had once admired it;

                               you could not have known
that the man walking with me,
my husband or brother, my father come home
from his aircraft carrier,
had his arm around me
to protect me.
That the way you greeted me —
     the punk slap on the back —
stung and hurt me,
that I was ignoring your violence,
not you,
when I walked away clinging to him,
refusing to speak to you.

Now I wake up
wanting to embrace you instead.
The rain that falls this morning is silver fish
from the sky. They fall
in shimmering heaps on the ground.
I drink my morning glass of water,
my husband still asleep in his tan body,
with his gardening, stone-lifting muscles coiled around him.
Inside my head
you have changed from your outrageous red shirt and green
        pants
into a conservative blue wool sweater and corduroy trousers,
are carrying books and just ready to put them down so that
you can touch me. The way you wanted to

when you slapped me
in the dream
instead.

I don't know who you are, except the world
you live in comes into my head
occasionally. Somehow,
it is my fault that you slapped me
when you really wanted to touch me
differently.
Even in my head
there is conflict between loving and possessing,
between men and women,
between love and I suppose
you have to call it
sex.
This morning you are the man I love most.

If that is the right word.

---

Quantum Reality #6: Neorealism (The world is made of or-
dinary objects.) An *ordinary object* is an entity which possesses
attributes of its own whether observed or not. With certain
exceptions (mirages, illusions, hallucinations), the world out-
side seems populated with objectlike entities. The clarity and
ubiquity of ordinary reality has seduced a few physicists — I call
them neorealists — into imagining that this familiar kind of reality
can be extended into the atomic realm and beyond. However,
the unremarkable and common-sense view that ordinary ob-
jects are themselves made of objects is actually the blackest heresy
of establishment physics.

"Atoms are not things," says Heisenberg, one of the high priests of the orthodox quantum faith, who likened neorealists to believers in a flat earth.

Nick Herbert, *Quantum Reality: Beyond the New Physics*

## SYLVESTER IN THE ARUGULA

My husband loves cats, and we have a wooden one
spiked into the arugula bed,
a black and white Sylvester, always sputtering,
as his mechanical legs stir in the wind,
never abandoning his diabolical plans to whap a paw down
     on Tweety Bird,
who always escapes this wooden ruffian with golf ball red
     nose,
feathers flying, unlike the occasional sparrows we find
     claws up
in the garden. Don't tell me you think I am a cartoon!

The boy with Tom Cruise voice laughed at my puffy
     mushroom
     white aerobic shoes, "I don't think they
     are funny," he said, "but they made me laugh when
I saw them." He's so thin I wonder what he eats;
but they are all thin, these beautiful boys
who write poems no one reads.

Sylvester in our garden: this is the world where Medea
    has become media, so that to me, Jason must sound
    like Tom Cruise because
    he/I too once "crashed and burned." His
    cover-of-*Time*-magazine picture hangs over
    my desk with the legend,
    "CRUISE CONTROL: Hollywood's top gun gets
        serious."
Yes, get serious, Diane, cruising through the images of
    California
    and its beach boys, the Palm trees and soft bare feet
    of suburban lawns. Playing $2 blackjack in Las Vegas,
    you dream of living in a casino hotel
    with neon lights that are never turned off.
Pick the last of this midwestern autumn arugula which
    Sylvester is
standing over. Wearing your cartoon shoes,
    can't you see that everything
    is a gamble, that it all
    might be a cartoon?
Maybe that's what Jason was laughing at,
    not the shoes, as he said, but how seriously
    you wear them.

At the same time that they led the way to Las Vegas, Angelenos led the rest of the country in creating the culture of the future. Other Americans retained more ambivalence about the promises of modernity, but Southern Californians embraced the future without hesitation. They incorporated moving pictures, theme amusement parks, automobiles, and other cultural advances into a new way of life for average citizens, and then transmitted the new styles to the rest of the country by way of such spectacle suburbs as Hollywood, Disneyland, and Las Vegas, where many Americans first encountered Southern California culture.

John M. Findlay, *People of Change*

The Ritter Cafe
Vienna

Dear Jonathan,

I suppose it's inevitable in this culture to hear the word "media" mistakenly for "Medea." Even though the accent is on a different syllable. Still the idea of "media" as a kind of sorceress is very appealing to me. The spells and enchantments which movies, TV, radio and magazines cast over us are not negligible.

In Creeley's poem "Kore," the haunting line "Oh, love, where are you leading me now?" is a reminder that we follow many things which we don't under stand. I suppose you could say they cast a spell over you. Or maybe we love and follow most things out of an invisible biological necessity, like migrating birds.

Yr Lady of Sorcery,

DW

# MEDIA, THE NEW SORCERESS

*for Robert Creeley*

How I have bragged all these years
that I do not read newspapers or watch television.
How I have opened my hands filled with moonlight
and found only human palms
which stretch into winter on the desert. But I am still the
        California Girl,
who grew up thinking life was the movies.

My neighbors in Michigan make their cactus bloom,
but even when I drive through America
looking for hawks on fence posts
and the flowers of prickly pear and barrel cactus,
teddy bear cholla or ocotillo, I find only myself.
Always thinking of the one man
for whom I gave up everything, my Jason
who laughed at me when he left me for another woman
saying I had misunderstood why he loved me,
that he only needed my magic,
that that other goddess, that slim footed one
had made me love him so much that nothing else mattered/
I was blinded with love.

These thick lenses which have
always covered my eyes,

they have hidden the real story from me.

But given me the power to see
something every Hollywood fan could tell you
is obvious: that we are the roles
we play, we become the words we speak.

Oh, silence, silence, or is it only
white noise? Steel Man pumps iron,
and I guess I pump light. Do I dream of
Tom Cruise in *Top Gun,* or Scott Glenn in *Silverado* or
John Cusack in *The Sure Thing,* I mean really dream,
when I am asleep and trying to forget about old age and
        death?
Or do the movements under my eyelids,
like sand rippling on the Mojave Desert, or which come
        on those
waves which are sound rather than light,

mean that I have turned into the words on printed pages and
like Medea escaping in her Chariot drawn by Dragons,
do I learn that no magic is powerful enough
to keep us from failing at love?

No magic can rescue any lover from betrayal. We can leave
behind everything we love and in doing so
we leave behind a story. The end of the story is not
death. It is escape. Beyond the story
is life, which we live, unlike stories
which happen to us and only in retrospect do we
tell, or live while we sleep. Of course, when Orpheus
        looks back
Eurydice is not there. Sorcery,

is only the diurnal movement. Night must
become day. Each morning, with the light, I open
my book and pour the steaming cup of coffee and begin
to feed myself with words, the ones which might carry me
beyond the body's betrayals.

Words, words,
where are you leading me now?

# STEAM

Rising from my black cup,
the Morning Glories imperceptibly turning their blue gulping
        mouths
towards me on the path I follow. There are landscapes
which refresh me. I come back to them
on mornings when my coffee unfurls in the garden air.
        Behind the
oaks,
the Pacific Ocean sometimes. But this morning,
it was Lake Tahoe, the air piney, the sense that you have
walking into a casino, that anything could happen.

I imagine more easily
sometimes,
the lives of others,
than my own. Heather who has the narrow hips
of a boy, wet-suit, skin-diver's legs, for instance
is drowning in a scene from her childhood, so I hold out
        my hand
Her father sits on a gold, crushed velvet couch
which swirls in her mind like a sandstorm. Her dark Brontë
        heroine
hair
is resisting the wind, like palm fronds,
as she refuses to climb onto Daddy's lap;
she's seen him packing an old navy blue duffel bag,

his toothpaste, she remembers his toothpaste, because
he should brush his teeth at home/his shaving cream, she
        should
find him
in the bathroom, with the cream spread over his face,
these tubes of white foam should not
be going into this nylon bag with the ragged cloth handle.
She thinks of this pain all the time, so I tell her to think
        of images,
not
feelings, but she thinks of when Daddy left,
the couch like the Mojave Desert,
uncrossable, no oasis for little girls,
his old duffel bag packed. He left her
to go to California and start over.

The clear air at Lake Tahoe makes me think of how
little girls love their daddies so much.
That same refreshing sense
that anything could happen. You've just sat down
at the blackjack table and bought a stack of chips, each one
fills your hand, as if you still had a child's hand.
It is a cookie, and now you must brush your teeth,
you've drunk your milk, time for bed,
Daddy will kiss you good night. I can't give
or take away these images. What I see is
the coffee still steaming as if we were sitting
at a picnic table under a pine looking at Lake Tahoe,
and Heather, walking across the sand she imagines
        California's full of.
And like a winner, each middle-aged summer day,
I count these Morning Glories,
stacked against the fence like big blue poker chips.

101

# BLACKJACK SESTINA

Twenty stories high above the desert
with its morning shadows, like the face of a woman wearing
a wide-brimmed hat, you stand quietly so that you won't
      wake
your husband, who sleeps like a tired gardener,
his hands brown from Michigan summer
labor—tomatoes, gypsy peppers, sweet basil and sun flowers.

You love this time of day when the hotel-bordering flowers,
—pansies like eyes and snap dragons like mouths—even
      in this desert,
hold dew. To some, this world is beyond summer;
but not to you, a California Girl who will grow old wearing
blue jeans and T-shirts. Your Beefmaster Tomato-gardener
husband loves this city of mirages later in the day, when
      it is awake,

But you love it in the morning light before others wake
up and drink their coffee. You are the gypsy flower
at the 6 a.m. blackjack table. Steel Man, husband-gardener
loves his Keno games, tends the numbers. You prefer to
      sit with these desert
cactus, old timers who've stayed up all night wearing
cigarettes growing inch-long ash from their mouths. Summer

long-gone, their wrinkled wintry hands stack up the chips.
        Summer
is a joke to them, here where they're always awake.

They've been around the clock; humor this Snapdragon-lady,
        who wearing
her night of sleep like a sprinklered flower,
sits down at their table in the early morning desert.
They know an inhospitable garden and its harsh gardener.

They know that Steel Man sleeping upstairs is not such a
        gardener.
They know hard summer;
her wide-brimmed hat shadowing her old face, Dame Desert
is a survivalist. They've learned this staying up all night,
        awake,
playing blackjack at basil green tables. They could be
        sunflowers,
big-rooted, heavy-headed, wearing

Sandy cigarette ash, which has fallen over them for hours;
        wearing
the cards like rows of seeds. She is their gardener.
They laugh at nursery-grown flowers
like me. Summer
snapdragons or pansies, newly awake
at 6 a.m. on their private desert.

A desert where they stay up all night wearing
tough, dusty foliage. I love to see Her wake in them, this
        gardener
of summer morning blackjack players, these old desert
        sunflowers.

# OCEAN

When I lived near the ocean
in languorous Laguna Beach, with miniskirts
and tanned legs, listening to the distant surf of drowned
     sailors
and the echo of my father's military mirror-shod feet
marching out the drum roll of rejection, "I'm leaving, I'm
     leaving,"

         "Oh, please don't go away,"

I did not walk that cobbled block down to Diver's Cove
every day as I had thought I would.

No more than once a week at most
did I wander on the beach, did I push myself against
     the wind
at low tide, look at sunsets, walk in the mists that blew
     in from the

                    foggy canyon.

I wanted to sit behind glass and look at the ocean all day
as if it were the mirror-shield some grey-eyed goddess gave
to a hero, one which had turned me, the monster,
     to stone.
I wanted to be so powerful
I could freeze all men

into love,
attention,
devotion. Like stone
they would have been,
fixed into the act of fulfilling me.

The secret is not why
I did not use my gaze, not that
I averted it to save the soft and mortal men
I loved, but that
my gaze has never had
that power. Goddesses are only
in the shape of women; they have not
borne children, or even seen the possibility
of aging. And goddesses become
something else. A secret I won't whisper even
to you, for if you follow me, you know it;
articulation would only confuse
the matter.

I have not wanted
to live my life; have wanted
to read about the lives which others
live. Emily Brontë, or Charlotte, walking on the moors,
encountering
the windy roll of green hills, plunging into
rough turfed, stony places with a bit of parkin
in their bags, to eat by a cotter's fire.

Beyond my oaks where I think I see
cottages and driveways:
the secret ocean like a mirror
some days. A silvered fish:
that's what I am,
a silvered lady of this ocean.

As many a European observed, it was not always easy for Americans to embrace the risks that they undertook. Gambling had less and less to do with social rank on the far western frontier, so one's stakes seemed more important to players in early California. "It is the money men gamble for here," explained Hubert Howe Bancroft late in the century, "and they have no hesitation in saying so." But bettors saw money increasingly as a measure of their participation rather than as just the goal of their play. Because gamblers behaved more predictably, relying on odds tilted infallibly in their favor, players increasingly understood that one could hardly get rich at betting. So while they continued to gamble for money, they did so in larger and larger part for the thrills that it provided. "It is a fine thing to get a peck or a bushel of gold just by betting for it," Bancroft realized, but "the tremulous rapture of mingled hope and fear is almost compensation enough even if one loses." Additionally, speedy games, and moderate stakes that prolonged participation, maximized excitement by intensifying the experience. "Next to the pleasure of winning is the pleasure of losing," the historian wrote: "only stagnation is unendurable."

John M. Findlay, *People of Chance*

The Ritter Cafe

Dear Jonathan,

In Robert Altman's film *The Player*, there's a
jewel-like scene which is also used in the trailer for
the film. Tim Robbins, as the amoral survivalist stu-
dio exec, is at one of his endless procession of lunches
where he drinks "power water," and he says (I para-
phrase), "Can't we talk about something other than
Hollywood? We're all educated people here, aren't
we?" There is a long pause, you almost think it's a
mistake, and you're going to hear the director yell
"Cut!", but then the face just breaks into one of
those Tim Robbins smiles, almost a laugh, and the
film cuts away to something else.

I wonder if it is possible for us "educated people" ever
to talk seriously about anything other than the obses-
sions of our daily need for love, sex, romance, money
and other trivial things? What is literature but a
discussion of how people go after those things and
usually fail, thus having to look for something else—
religion, poetry, philosophy. I have come to love the
Romantic Comedy genre of Hollywood movies as I
never thought I would because I believe that we are
seeing, in a film like *Pretty Woman* the essence of

what philosophy, religion and certain poetry offers us—a way to soothe our fears with hope and possibility of trivial things like Romantic love, and of course, joy.


Yr Lady of the Silver Screen,

DW

## LIGHT CAP

Remember the scene
in *King Solomon's Mines,* the movie
where Deborah Kerr who has been grubby
and swaddled against beauty on the long march
into Africa, washes her red hair, at the waterfalls,
and when it dries, suddenly she is
an angel? Her hair on fire, glowing her
(Hollywood) beauty
out
to Stewart Granger, lean, Abercrombie and Fitch garbed
in khaki, lighter than his tan.

She is suddenly
light headed
in his presence, not
just her beauty,
but her woman-self spiraling out
like a soft skein of embroidery silk/
that movie from my adolescence imprinting me
with an image of what love should be—the man, rugged and powerful,
suddenly in the power of the woman as she reveals
her light.

In a London newspaper, seen in the airport,
there was a photo of Stewart Granger, probably aged 75/
　　　more?
who would know the weathered, somewhat hefty face
as that lean-visaged explorer we women
fantasized?
　　　　　Aging seems so obvious;
　　　　　why doesn't death become a logical conclusion?

We live in an age when
understatement, implied conclusions,
are the most artful. I say you should see the woman,
from the back (as she looks seventeen), walking on
the beach, and then see nothing
but the ocean, the sandpipers running
like mechanical toys, the surf like lace on a party dress,
the black rocks shiny with the spume, as patent leather. You
should imply on-going beauty, an infinite ending,
inhuman, immortal, a movie
which could last longer even
than the celluloid.

Everything mirrored
in waterfalls, or an
ocean.


# DRIVING BARBARA'S SHORE


First, there's the slight tinge,
a raw flesh odor, to the air when you
drive off the freeway in Santa Monica towards the
Pacific Ocean. The green on this clear morning, is only
        deckled
at the edges with white,
as you turn north on the highway, and glide
along the shore towards Point Dume,
towards Santa Barbara, continuing to skirt the Pacific
in a green car which curves and dips and curls with
        the road's
meander. There is someone riding the waves
in black suit
out there, in touch with tunnels of water.
The black asphalt road
wraps my female body here on the shore; and
for a moment I think I hear
salt talking to me, green water
sluicing my shoulders, some
sound I learned to listen for when I was a child,
in my black high-topped shoes,
holding seashells to my ear,
after a day building with wet sand, and

eating white bread sandwiches at the beach. Something
which made me not want to put on my shoes or go home
after my shoulders were sunburned like carnations, made me
look out at the ocean
and think,
"if I could stay here,
the day might never end."

---

The Cafe Eau de Vie
East Lansing

Dear Jonathan,

You are across the Atlantic in Europe. Craig is two
thousand miles to the West, on the edge of the
Pacific, and I am here in the American Midwest with
Steel Man and a million young Jasons. Here I con-
stantly face the fact that it is my longing to be
somewhere else, my fantasy of what life could be,
that is the light, the flame. I love to look through
the oak trees in our tiny back yard and think that in-
stead of Grove Street being on the other side of them,
they are hiding a view of the Pacific Ocean. Poetry
makes all of this possible.

---

# SUDDEN MENDENHALL GLACIER

The oaks which are suddenly covered with a glacier
of malachite leaves, now freeze me
away from my neighbors,
the view of the Midwest backyards,
white clapboard, shingle roofs
I have in winter. Now I can imagine
that there is a different world
just a block away. The Pacific Ocean
shushing against the rocks at Point Sur
or the Oregon Coast, building frosted curls
for surfers at Corona del Mar. I can imagine that
my friend Norman, on Oahu, and I, in Michigan, share
two sides of the Pacific, and if we could look across several
        thousand
miles, see each other, out of our windows. Or my friend
        Craig could
be driving along the Coast Highway to Zuma, and I would
        almost hear
his pirate Beatles tapes harmonizing him towards bikinied
        girls. I
don't know why I like to imagine that the Pacific Ocean
        is just
beyond my backyard fence, or why the Mendenhall green
        foliage
gives the illusion of collapsing space. Like time,
trapped into glacier ice, water frozen and holding artifacts

from eons ago, the space between Midwest and West coast
condensed behind this green mass, exists as
imagination, or residue.
                              My critics say
I don't have the zest, the bare leg, the cutting
jag of breath of my bohemian youth, but I say
it is all there, condensed into my short frosty hair
and the sad but accepting words Medea utters
after the tragedy, and she has flown to Athens to lead
a more sedate and royal life. I say that space and time
condense; exist as the imagined Pacific Ocean just beyond
        my Oaks
here in the Midwest; are the residue
like feral bones in a glacier
of life forms past, perhaps even now
extinct.

---

I used to chafe in Michigan. But I scarcely do any
more. Still, I keep wondering whether I could have a
better life if I hadn't chosen to hide away in this
obscure location. Did I choose it? Or was it my
destiny? I do owe, in part, the Michigan eyes that I
have acquired to my sophisticated French friend, An-
nette Smith, who when she came to visit a few years
ago, took a walk with me. As we were walking back
to the house from the university campus, she said,
"All these years you have told me what a drab and
dreary place you live in, but this is a (French accent)
"vee-lahge," a charming "vee-lahge." Actually, now

113

that we have a few espresso cafes and several good
book stores, this has begun to be true. Or maybe it's
just that I have Michigan eyes, thanks to Annette.

Yr Lady of the Village of East Lansing,

DW

# THE SILKY ISLANDS

Each Sunday we leave our little house
with its combination of tidy
and untidy rooms, the shiny floors like commercial seashells,
and the worn carpets like old bathing suits,
to walk to the village cafe where they serve espresso
and sell the Sunday edition of *The New York Times.* We get
a table by the window, often next to the local journalist
who wears a trench coat just as if he were a film noir
        reporter,
and who usually has his laptop computer on the table
with its black canvas carrying case,
like a diplomat's pouch, lying on the chair next to him.
    I fetch myself a glass of water, wipe off the table,
            organize
our chairs, and Steel Man goes

to the bar to get my single
espresso and his big glass of cafe latte
while I dissect the paper, separating out the delectable
organs—the *Book Review* tabloid, the Art and Leisure
  section, the
glossy
magazine, and of course the Travel section—from the
  body:
  the news, business, other irrelevant stuff we
  throw away.
       I try not to remember
the mornings of a summer long ago on the island
of Hydra with a handsome monster who drank Nescafe
while I had my tea and read the international edition of
the *Herald Tribune.* Or other times in my life
when the world seemed to rumble around me like a volcano
which I couldn't hear. Oh, but the heat/I knew it was
out there/no, underneath me! waiting to spew out liquid
  rock
and moving embers, trap me, vaporize me, only I wouldn't
  even
turn into an archaeological relic, like Pompeii, whose dress
  or shoes
or bracelet, now transmogrified into stone, might be the
  subject of a
learned
paper on customs or social status of women in the late 20th
  century.


Sitting in the winter sun of this window
at our Cafe Venezia, I read
about a poet who nobody remembers already,
even though he probably isn't dead. My ashy blond hair
is on fire as I sip from my white porcelain cup
black volcanic coffee, alternating with mouthfuls of clear

water, and I thought that if only my life didn't have to
        be lived
but only written about, and I could read about myself
        each day
instead
of enacting the drama, how superior that would be; I
        might be
lying on the beach next to the clear water of the
        Mediterranean
getting a tan on my blond body, one which would not turn
        into skin
cancer,
and dipping my hand into the cool and rubbing it across
        my hot
sweaty shoulders.
        All these surfaces,
                all experienced sequentially,
yet none particularly sequential.
                I am not sure any more
about the function of intelligence, whether it produces better
    results than stupidity. All surfaces turn into
        interiors, then return to
the surface. Ocean, coffee,
        my life in the Village of East Lansing.

# FOREIGN TRAVEL

We were in the trendy clothing store where everything
    looks slightly
used, but still costs a substantial price.
I tried on a pair of women's Wing Tip shoes, black. They
    weren't
long and pointed, Zoot-suitish, as they should be
for anything so improper to a woman.
Robert said you look like someone trying to be a lesbian
but not understanding sexuality.
I said, yes, they're not absurd enough. Women should
look like clowns when they wear conventional
men's clothing. These make me look like
I want to be a man, but instead I
have just become a wimp.


We looked at saddle bags, either made out of fake leather or
inexpensive leather. We looked at Doc Martens, all in little
sizes. Robert wears a twelve.
We looked at rumpled but expensive and not really great
men's jackets. I looked at hats which all looked better
on their pegs than on my head. We looked at famous
photographs made into cards. Searching
for Elvis, but only finding Marilyn
Monroe. We

looked at coffee mugs, large ones
knowing that we own almost
fifty-seven coffee
cups plus twenty-
four demi-
tasses
which we never use.
Look behind you, Robert says,
as I am fingering velvet
bags. The redhead
with the green shoes. How pointed they are. That's how
        those Wing
Tips should be.
I look at the
green suede shoes
on her student-feet.
They are not more pointed
than the Wing Tips.
But they are a shade of green
no oxford shoe was ever meant
to be. They don't look zany either.
Maybe it's that store. Nothing looks crazy
in that store. We like it though. Feel accomplished
when we leave without buying anything.

It's like a foreign country. A place where, when you
        arrive,
the hotel accommodations are uncomfortable, the bathroom
        terrible,
the food never as good as the food at home. You can't speak
the language, you don't know what's going on. You realize
        your only purpose
in going there is to buy something. Foreign travel is just a
        shopping
trip. You buy things because they look odd, or

interesting or typical of that country. You get home and
        hope you
have friends or relatives you can give these purchases to
        as gifts.
You certainly
don't/can't use most of them. What looked enchanting or
        odd in the
foreign shops, looks shoddy, or improbable when you are
        home in
America. You realize the Wing Tip shoes would have looked
        just as ugly
or stupid on your feet if they had had long pointed toes, as
        they do
being imitation men's shoes for women. The girl with the
        green shoes
looks normal in this store, like a foreigner herself.
Maybe those shoes were normal
in a Baltic country. In here they
look sort of normal too but her green shoes probably just
        look ugly
when she leaves the shop. If you see her on the street
you'd say, "why would anyone want to wear green
        oxfords?" Not,
"wow, look at those shoes" the way Robert said to you,
on the street after you left the store:
        "look, Edward Scissorhands!" and you look and see a
        tall boy
    with a black cape and extraordinary hair, long but
            puffed and
        teased and kind of half sticking out of his head. Wearing
    normal men's Wing Tips, of course.
Once we leave the store I ask
myself why I am trying to save up money for a trip abroad.
All I would do is shop/I can do that in Ann Arbor, Michigan

119

# SALT-FREE TALK

*For Norman Hindley, who sent me some*
*peppercorns called "Paradise"*

He'll never have a medical problem/you can
see it,
    in the healthy body,
        good skin color, firm flesh
            even when he doesn't exercise,
                clear eyes, etc.
                  I mean,
a medical problem
    connected with his salt consumption.

I can't believe it sometimes,
seeing him cover everything with salt
before he's even tasted
the food, and now that he eats
and cooks lots of Oriental-style dishes, the
flagon of soy sauce is always on the table before his plate,
and that
covers everything, sometimes even the salad
liberally.

A few times in fifteen years, I have heard him say
"it's too salty," of a dish I have prepared. Sometimes when
    it didn't

even
taste salty to me, I the woman who hardly ever salts
at table. Which has led me to believe that it is
not salt he tastes, but something else, for the salt itself
is consumed, almost breathed as if it were air,
a normal requirement for common functioning.

His sense of humor is like the salt, daily,
and I breathe it like air, a necessity for daily
consumption, something I would only notice if it were
        missing.
It is sprinkled over our conversation throughout a day
without even thinking, and the extra flask of it like *shoyu*
is always there by the plate to darken and spice
the healthier style of our life together.

People say I am mellower than I used to be.
I say my life is happier, more comfortable, different.
Do I see my past life as a rather amusing soap opera, or even
        my present
longings for teenage love, sex and romance or young Pulitzer
        Prizes
or not to die, as everyday jokes, sprinkled like Steel Man's
        salt and soy
over every vision of myself?

I have a theory about his
salty tastes. A heavy smoker since childhood
he needs very sharp tastes, many subtle ones elude him.
I too have no way of accepting my daily humanness.

It seems tasteless, insipid, but like Steel Man, I lavishly
        sprinkle it
with stinging wit, or

absurdity. With jokes,
usually at my own expense. And it
tastes good.

My mother in her nursing hospital
with swollen legs, ulcerated and bleeding,
from sitting, sitting, and eating small meals of
Campbell's soup which must be almost entirely composed
of salt—oh, spare me world
from that destiny, to be old like my mother, complaining
and bitterly about how no one loves her
and how tasteless the food is
because they will not give her
any salt.

My father was a sailor, the salty ocean was his life.
He left my mother, he left me, and Old Salt took on some
          meaning
I cannot shake. Am I the pepper then,
to my husband's salt? Burning, dark,
paradise grains which take bland white flesh,
marbled red meats or crisp green vegetables and snapshot
          spice into
their daily texture?

---

According to the orthodox ontology, before a measurement
occurs, all of an unmeasured electron's possibilities are live
possibilities: just before it strikes the screen, the electron is not
headed in a particular direction. If we must talk about it at

all, just before it hits, the electron is headed everywhere at once. The rule of the road for unmeasured electrons is this: a single quon takes all paths.

Nick Herbert, *Quantum Reality: Beyond the New Physics*

---

## POINT DUME

The runner, walking next to me
gave up sports when he went to college.
His stepping is crooked, like a tree branch,
        An alcoholic can't ever again
have even one beer,
though he longs for it like a dowser,
pointing a branch for water.
        I cannot touch
the keyboard again, my fingers winter
twigs.
        No use
to say, the sons are branches,
their father the sea.
            No use to say
you gave up everything and now
have nothing. There never was a bargain,
only salty faith. Only the possibility
of finding sweet water.

# LOTTO NIGHT

On the ocean, I think.
On the ocean. I would like to live
on the ocean. In a house which would seem
as if it were in an ad for rum. Remember,
I lived at the ocean once,
only a block away from the Pacific,
a grey glimpse like the shining edge of a gopher snake
disappearing in the orchard could be seen from one window.

But the nights were hollow, my life
damper than the fog, and the men who played Frisbee
on the beach by day turned into vampires
at night. I heard the tap dance studio clattering
down the alley from the rosebushes,
and I didn't know why my hands
seemed translucent when standing on the beach.

There is something colder than the ocean's breath,
something which drowned sailors can talk about, but which
is a test for mariners who must be the sanest of men,
not ever paying attention to ghosts or foggy voices.
My father was a sailor, a hearty image playing cribbage
with matchstick counters, his ruddy face
I now know to have been red
with the rich blood of a night watchman,

someone who couldn't be frightened by mist
or fog. I love him, even now, because he was so fearless.

And I am drawn to the ocean, I want to live
by the ocean, I want to look at its silvery lidded cover
and think about my stout father
who laughed ghosts with white hair away,
who reminds me that I have two sets of genes,
not just the ghostly ones of my moonlit hair,
but his darker ones, the ones which can stand in the fog
and do not wince when something invisible,
like your past
brushes by. Do I need to win the lotto
to buy a house overlooking the water when it might turn
    into
the house I already lived in? The one near the ocean,
whose bonds I escaped from, though perhaps there are still
wisps, like fog, that cling to my wrists or ankles?
Oh, thank you, Redneck Father,
thank you, always in your cap of darkness
standing watch outside this penniless house.


# MY HEROES HAVE ALWAYS
# BEEN COWBOYS


The man I hadn't seen for so many years
recently found me at a public event
and presented me with two hybrid roses
in a glass of water.

125

When I knew him, he
played the cello and had
the voice of a radio star.
Scarecrow thin in his tux,
spatulate fingers,
the boy on the sea,
Newport Beach of rich

doctors' houses, the camellias
glowing in Fourth of July water. Loved me
from a distance, he said,
while loving men
up close.

It never occurred to me
to love him, though he grew the
most beautiful roses. Played music
I would love to make love to—Schubert,
Vivaldi, Mozart. And besides,
he was dying when he said
he'd always loved me—

from a distance. Death makes
all worldly love seem more
believable than it usually is
or was. Sheer Bliss was the name
of one of the roses he brought me. Like a score
for the cello, the petals offered a perfect
pattern.

He knew my heroes had
always been cowboys, and though he
was probably capable of loving Willie Nelson,
though not Tammy or Dolly or Loretta,
his idea of American music was
Robert Craft conducting Stravinsky.

126

You tell me you see pain in my face,
saw it when we were gambling in Las Vegas,
saw it in the video tape I sent you from Phoenix.
I don't think of it much since I live so happily with
    Steel Man,
but when we get older, our faces lose their opaque
creamy rose petal or magnolia tough thick textures. You
    must see
the bloody remains of my past shining through
my newly translucent face.
When you look at me you can see I have
accepted responsibility for having eaten that fruit,
the golden orange on the Tree in my youth.

And neither he, nor anyone else, can tempt me now
with roses or love from a distance.
Even if my heroes had not
always been cowboys,
I would have ridden away
from that terrible garden of men who only love men,
on my high horse—that magic horse—
long ago.

## WATER, MIRRORS

There is a corridor
I don't want to walk down.
I always thought I would, the one
Cocteau so compelling visualized for all

of us, with human arms and hands
as wall brackets, holding the light for La Belle,
as she searched not for The Beast, but
Jean Marais, when he was young
so breathtakingly handsome, oh how we
want all ugliness transformed into
the simplest set
of possibilities.

There is a corridor
which is lined with blood
that is rotting, or tainted. I won't
watch vampire movies, or other horror films.
I know they are the place the corridor
leads to. I know they are worse
than falling out of the window of a skyscraper
and smashing your body on a city street, worse than
falling and crushing your body from a water tower
or the Matterhorn.

There is a corridor
which I have to walk some nights
just to be alive in the mornings. No wonder
I welcome the first light of day. No wonder I love
the Silver Screen image of Golden Navarre on his black horse
who's back in his human form after another diurnal passage
as the black wolf, now holding out his glove for the
          Ladyhawk.
No wonder I hear just before dawn, in my sleep, the whisper
"La Belle, La Belle," as I know that I am in
the corridor, and it is leading me away
from any love or truth as I once imagined it,
but also leading me away
to be safe again in my old woman
guise, for another day, another passage.

There is a corridor
I don't want to walk down,
but some nights I am given no choice.
The beast is growling at the dinner table,
my hands are turning into claws, taloned, scaly
and sharp. Will I escape because I was
never the beauty? Why do I hear those voices,
along the corridor, whispering my name as if it were a spell,
not "La Belle, La Belle" but
"Diane, Diane," the syllables rise like heartbeats.
I hurry through the soft blooded walls,
morning and light through the windows, to hear my safe
        husband
saying,
"Diane, Diane,"
and I open my eyes
to a small house without corridors.

"Don't you have
to get up this morning?"

---

Colored objects have an intrinsic color; black objects don't. Heat
up a black object, however, and it begins to glow. Steel makers
for generations gauged furnace temperatures by this black-body
glow. They know, for instance, that iron turns cherry-red
around thirteen hundred degrees. For physicists the black-body
puzzle is how to calculate the color of that glow at different
temperatures.

A black object is made of little pieces of matter. Whenever these
pieces move, they shake waves into their attached elec-
tromagnetic fields—waves our eyes interpret as colored light.

The faster the particles move, the higher the frequency of the light that is shaken off. As an object gets hotter, its parts move faster. That's the sort of thinking that goes on in a classical physicist's head as he sets out to calculate the color of black-body glow.

Classical physicists had little idea of the nature of the light-emitting particles in a block of hot iron but they assumed that, like everything else in the world, they obeyed Newton's laws. Today we know that light is caused by moving electrons. However, not only do electrons not follow classical laws, they do not even follow a classical *kind* of law—that is, a law that governs the motion of real objects.

Nick Herbert, *Quantum Reality: Beyond the New Physics*

## VIENNESE COFFEE

Wearing a coat of whipped cream whiteness
    drinking a steaming paper cup of coffee
    waiting for a train in a station which unfolds and unfolds,
    like a map on thick paper, crackling in our cold hands.

Wearing a long crow-black wool overcoat,
    the hot coffee in its cardboard container
    making stem rise out of your wet gloves,
    is the only thing we share, you black, I white,
    in our outer garments.

Beethoven wrote and wrote his black-noted
    espresso rich sonatas and symphonies
    in this city, and Mozart played zanily
    as he rushed underground, but I ignored pain
    in this city, and wonder now if Viktor Frankl and others
    like Hitler didn't set in motion some axis
    that requires all who come here to be able
    to survive. Some the punishers and torturers,
    others the receivers of pain. I, who had previously spoken
    of betrayers, how could I have known
    the scorpion "M" would betray me even while
    we were visiting this city, I in the opera watching
    La Boheme, he trailing young men
    down the snowy streets even into the Austrian Alps.
    The worst of betrayers, opening his body
    like a tomb, making me wonder ever after if sex
    were only for the depraved. Ah, city of Nazis, you offered
    some answers to that question, didn't you?

The train stations hold fathers and mothers, also
    with their paper cups of hot coffee,
    and in my memory it is with a kind friend that I am
            standing,
    as I leave for another city alone. He is the man
    in the dark coat, and I visited him without
    the snake coiling around my collar.
    This coffee the only blackness.
    Night a time for sleep,
    the morning fresh as a star,
    the paled out moon setting, and this evening
    a Strauss opera, Rosenkavalier. Joy, love that is
    shared, the only trickery results in fun.
    I am an old fashioned woman,
    not one who believes
    that love and death go together.

The Ritter Cafe
Vienna

Dear Jonathan,

My memories of Michael and his secret homosexuality, my stupidity, blindness I suppose, still torture me. I think of myself as so perceptive, but miss truth when it is too painful. Like everyone else. I look in the mirror constantly, thinking that if I can understand myself, I can understand the world. What I want to see is the twin of myself, as a completion. But that is deceptive too. Magicians and mirrors. Illusion replaces image.

Oh, mirrors. *The Blood of a Poet.* Anyone who imagines is a twin, an incestuous twin, her male self bursting through the mirror, like Cocteau's poet to get on the other side of reality. The other half of the Orpheus-self is Eurydice, the lover and beloved, the male and female, all parts of the twin whole. The mirror offers a representation of this. The cinema is, as Paglia claims, the natural culmination of "the aggressive Western eye," though any camera will do. Beauty and narcissism are dangerously intertwined. Or so it has seemed to me in my life. As you know, I have never been able to accept men who love other men. What I love about men is not men-ness, but the fact that they are the other half of me. Conversely, the other half of a man should be a woman. This is what Catherine, in *Wuthering Heights,* feels about Heathcliff. But then look at all the trouble that caused!

This poem is for one of my Troubadours, who is a twin. He hates his twin-ness, as if it is a limit, rather than an image of multiple possibilities. He was a baseball player, than a dancer until he hurt his back. He told me once that he hated mirrors. He has a gift for poetry but at present is not using it. He is an interesting enigma to me.

## THE DEER IN ME

*Gary Snyder's poem "Long Hair" offers the idea that the deer choose the hunters who shoot them, and by getting the hunters to eat them, they live inside them to create the "revolution from within."*

When you couldn't dance any more
you wondered if words could replace the
muscles in your body?
First in your eyes where I
saw them swimming as if irretrievably
into Balboa's blue Pacific
then as winter sleeves, snowy,
covering until they melted, clear and trans-

parent, into your long arms, stretching
stretching, first you'd lay them across parts
of your dancer's body, as if draping them for an
impromptu costume, then wearing them into tatters,
until they must have disappeared after they had worn
their patterns into your skin.

My own body: I've never danced anywhere
except in my head. My silvery, moonlit hair
creating a phosphorescent glow as I bobbed through
my darkened life. Sometimes I put silver shoes
on my short chunky feet but poor woman that I am,
I could never follow a partner. Even though I was not
good enough to be a soloist,
I could only dance alone. So, there is my story.

But what if I too
could make my words, like silver arrows,
like tinsel, like glittering icicles, like strings of
water on spider webs or silver finger bowls
dance and clatter over my body,
until they draped into soft costume?
What if I too could suck them so close
that they'd vaporize with heat
and pass through my skin into my body—
this silver of lover's words—
until every pore absorbed
them, until I was muscled
in my whole body,
not just my head, with words.

I don't think you understand your own power.
You come from double-ness,
body and mind, equal in symmetry.
Unlike me, tiger, tiger, burning bright,

vaporizing the body, as I try to transform words
into motion, my head like a ball of mercury,
beautiful, deadly silver drop.

*for Chris Mandenberg*

The Rose Diner

Dear Craig,

I was intrigued with John Mathias' surprise that your
poetry is so different from mine. Nobody must think
we have any brains! They seem to think that the only
way people can be involved is to be clones. How can
anyone think that I would love a poet who is a clone
of me? Isn't that one of the things I rejected about
motherhood? Isn't that the greatest punishment my
mother inflicted on me as a child—to constantly tell
me I was exactly like her? I know you and I enjoy
our similarities, but surely our differences are just as
important. Perhaps more important.

Why am I such a rabid heterosexual? It's because the
kind of love I believe in can only exist between op-
posites. Otherwise, it is just narcissism, self love.
That's what most parental love is. Narcissism. It's just
looking in the mirror, not breaking through it to the
other side. Well, of course, there is nothing wrong
with healthy self love. It's all in the balance. We need
to love ourselves AND to love otherness. But if you
do love yourself, you don't need a carbon copy out

135

there, do you? I could write a whole book on the twin-couples in *Wuthering Heights*—Hindley and Nellie, Catherine and Heathcliff, Edgar and Isabella, Hareton and Cathy. Of course Catherine can't marry Heathcliff. They are twin mirror-images of each other. She understands this, but he does not. Interesting.

Perhaps this kind of love, which is so much an extension of oneself that it seems to be twin-like, or mirror-imaging, is religious? I am not sure that this will make more sense if I try to explain, so I'll leave it at that. However, I do think it explains our love of certain kinds of movie stars. I think about movie stars often, as does everyone in this culture. I don't so much long for them or envy them as think about how they represent the life simultaneously lived and not-lived. I watch so many movies now that I feel personally involved with actors and actresses sometimes. Have you ever seen a quite astonishing film called *A Town Like Alice*? This meditation came about when I started asking myself why I like the Australian actor, Bryan Brown so much. I decided that it might be the same thing I like about Steel Man, my husband: the big shoulders. So comforting and attractive at the same time.

Yr lady of the Silver Screen,

DW

# SHOULDERS

(Meditating on the Australian Actor
Bryan Brown, after Seeing
*A Town Like Alice*)

What do actors do
when they go home at night?
If they have wives, do they think
their wives love them
for any reason different?
— their surfaces, their acres of brown
   muscled arm, their legs which
   look as good as chocolate, in shorts,
   the green eyes which look into the camera
   quizzically, as if they are the velvet of a panther
   in a cage, looking at you without acknowledging he's
   behind bars.

The camera must be
a set of invisible bars,
yet you both imagine melting
through them.

What does an actor do
after he's been a man crucified,
his hands nailed to a barracks wall
by brutal Japanese soldiers in Malaysia,

all because he stole some chickens for a girl
he admired, who was nearly starved and broken
by these same Japanese soldiers. And the girl,
after the war, finds out in fact he isn't dead
and takes off to find him. How can an actor who
acts the role of a man who
has loved a woman enough to be crucified for her
go home at night and not feel inadequate
because he doesn't love his wife enough,
or anyone
enough to be
crucified for them? That kind of courage
isn't in our modern world any more. It has evolved away,
which is why we love to see movies about it, something
          from
the past we no longer have. Or how can he go home at
night after he has spent the day portraying a photographer
for *National Geographic* who loves a woman who gives up
          her whole
life to try to save gorillas, who knows she loves him, but
          will not
give up one animal she might save, for human love and is
murdered in her bed by some angry man. Loving
these woman on the screen,
surely that would make him feel
that the actual woman he lives with
does not have much substance. She's been shopping
in London or Beverly Hills, maybe studying her own script
for a movie, or planning a dinner party. He has the
muscles, like bags of nuts he's pumped up into his chest and
shoulders, his arms ripple when he unlocks the elegant door
          of his
house, and he must look at her with the same quizzical
expression in his green eyes that he offers the camera,
          when she

says "Hi, how did things go today."
She doesn't say, "how was the crucifixion?"
or "did the guerrillas piss on anyone today?" She's
not silly. But how does he know that she loves
him, or docs he in fact love her? He wouldn't be crucified
for anyone, if he could help it. No one would.


On the other hand, why is the actor
with his face like an Easter Island carving
or his arms and legs like the pistons of some steam engine
or his eyes as green as the water around the Great Barrier
        Reef
less likely to be loved because of,
and despite these things, simultaneously?


I see my husband across a hotel lobby, coming towards me
and it is the carved face,
        the shoulders rippling big cat-like
        under his jacket,
        a salty ocean of a man,
        his size-12 feet with the delicate ankles so common to
                                        handsome men


that I loved
before I knew anything else about him.
Actors are not beguiling us,
or fooling us with their surfaces.


No more than anything mortal.


The camera's never off
until we're dead.

Loving is always fantasy,
and no, there is no way to know
what you would offer of yourself
when that fantasy
is challenged.

## SILVER COYOTE SONG

(In the Spirit of Jerry Rothenberg)

Well and what were you doing in the woodshed?
Well and what does a fox need with wood?
Well and no, I see you are not a fox.
Well and maybe you are related to a fox.

There is a voice which I heard
in the Southern California hills, when
the gopher snake stretched itself like a branch
across the road, when I ate oranges whose thick skins
were smudged with soot from the earlier cool nights.
Not like wolves, or dogs. Not my father's voice
when he returned across the front yard from his battleship.

The moon has a voice like a silver charm bracelet
and though California is the Golden State, the trail I left
there is silver, slippery like the sled marks of mollusks, and I
heard the moon every night whispering twisted foil
messages. Coyotes in the hills
everyone said, but the voice I heard
had nothing to do with tricks or lobo smiles.

Well and what was he doing
riding his silver motorcycle to your door?
Well and who spoke your name, since you spoke his
with your silver charm bracelet voice?
Well and I don't believe that coyote,
whatever he tells me, Well and I don't
believe in your Silver Surfer either.

There is a voice, that's all I can say.
Silver baby shoes, the only charm. Silver
when you open your eyes. Silver
when the coyote slips behind the pepper tree
and runs ashy, grey-eyed, or invisible
away from your yard.
Well and why is this ghost of light always present?
Well and who follows the motorcycle
leaving a vapor of silver feathers in the night?

## A DIFFERENT EDGE

(In Response to a Poetry Student Who
Asked What Happens to Artists That
Makes Them "Lose Their Edge" as They Age)

What you wanted to
say,
was: "listen to me."

What you wanted
to say,
was: "listen to me."

And what I did not know how to say
then
to you
was this:
   it never changes.
   There is only an edge
   if you want to perceive
   an edge.
What I could not find words to say
to you
was this:
   it does not matter who listens to you,
   or whether you think you have the cutting edge
   or not. If you
   believe in what you have to say,
   letting nothing stop you from
   saying it.
   History will decide,
   finally. Even
   with our historical perspectives,
   we don't know
   what
   history will decide.
What I could not say to you because it
sounded so middle-aged
was this:
   you would not recognize an
   edge
   if you saw it.
   None of us would.
   None of us.

That's why
it doesn't matter.
Everything is surrounded. Nothing
in this world is not
surrounded. Edges
are perception.
Keep the faith.
Do what you believe in.
If you cared
about beauty,
if you cared about
beauty more than history, fame or influence,
it would not matter
to you
who listened.

This is my failing:
I have cared who listened.
How many listened.
This is history,
not art.
Even this line
drawn between you and me
is history, not
art.

Beauty
is not about anything.
It will not prevent death.
It carries its own meaning,
like a cell,
complete yet not final.

# PANDAS

Always wearing black, with his smooth
Korean face a mask, his rounded eyes never
showing me anything but attention, he politely
waits
for me to finish talking.
Opens his briefcase,
looks at his pack of Benson & Hedges —
it was just a reflex,
he closes the case.

"I used to collect pandas." He almost smiles.
I smile. This is the first sign of life he's shown.
Except looking briefly in the case at the cigarettes
before remembering his mask.

My office on the third floor in a corner
cul de sac is nearly empty.
I've gutted the files,
given away stacks of books and magazines,
pledged the wooden desk lemony.
Drink Price of Wales tea from a high-fired
clay mug, as a panda bear sits
holding his briefcase on his black-trousered lap
silently waiting in this remote office for my approval.
"Endangered," I say, or do I think it?
His facade so obvious.

This black and white clad boy
allows me to part the foliage. What do I glimpse
for a moment? The black and white, endangered panda edge
of poetry?

---

The Ritter Cafe
Vienna

Dear Jonathan,

The Jasons of my life—they've all been men who
radiated something. Light, I guess. Why else am I so
interested in quantum physics, a study of light, one
might say. Or so happily married to a photographer,
a man who manipulates light. So, let me share this
passage from *Sexual Personae* which has been singing
to me all day.

---

Early Christianity first uses the Greek work *charisma* ("gift,
favor, grace") for the gift of healing or speaking in tongues.
But I view charisma as completely pre-Christian. Athena gives
charisma to Achilles when she sheds "a golden mist around his
head" and makes his body emit "a blaze of light." She gives
charisma to Odysseus on Phaeacia: he becomes "taller and stur-
dier"; his hair thickens like "the hyacinth in bloom"; he is "ra-
diant with comeliness and grace." Xenophon says the beauty
of a victorious athlete, like "the sudden glow of a light at night,"
"compelled everyone to look at him": "Beauty is in its essence

145

something regal." Charisma in classical antiquity meant exactly what it does in the pagan mass media: glamour, a Scottish word signifying, as Kenneth Burke points out, a magic "haze in the air" around persons or things. Charisma is the numinous aura around a narcissistic personality. It flows outward from a simplicity or unit of being and a composure and controlled vitality. There is gracious accommodation, yet commanding impersonality. Charisma is the radiance produced by the interaction of male and female elements in a gifted personality. The charismatic woman has a masculine force and severity. The charismatic man has an entrancing female beauty. Both are hot and cold, glowing with presexual self-love.

Camille Paglia, *Sexual Personae*

---

I think that describes the image of my father, unexpectedly coming home on furlough from WW II, young and handsome in his naval uniform, walking through the palm tree sunset—what a fairy tale image this Cinderella-Diane has longed for. Men are always magic, a surprise to me.

Yr Lady Who Loves Light,

DW

# MOVING THE CHAIR

I forget how differently
men do things, from women.
At least in the world I prefer. So,
it surprises me to see him move the chair
away from, yes the rather awkward genteel place where
I've put it. He swings it comfortably over his
tall body, around to the other side
of the table, negotiating in a very small space
with perfect control. Puts the chair in a place
where he can lean his elbows on the table,
concentrate.

It surprises me
in the way it might surprise me
if he had suddenly put his arms around me,
to rescue me,
if I were walking without notice
as I often do, and a door were about to hit me.

It surprises me to realize
this physical control. I know I love it
when I watch dancers, and I think I know this
when I think about sex,
but what I always forget
is its daily force in certain men.
They are there to hold you

when you might fall. They can
make the world more comfortable
just by being able to swing a chair over
their heads and place it perfectly
in a spot you hadn't realized
was even there.

---

A visitor to Niels Bohr's country cottage asked him about a
horseshoe nailed above the front door. "Surely, Professor Bohr,
you do not really believe that a horseshoe over the entrance
to a home brings good luck?" "No," answered Bohr, "I cer-
tainly do not believe in this superstition. But you know," he
added, "they say it brings luck even if you don't believe in it."

Nick Herbert, *Quantum Reality: Beyond the New Physics*

---

The Rose Diner

Dear Craig,

Of course, the man in my life who most fulfilled that
Jason role was the man who became my so-called
Motorcycle Betrayer. He wasn't a sailor though, and
in the real sense, neither was my father. He was just
enlisted in the Navy.

However, there was a man in my life who was a genuine sailor. He was my mentor, David Smith who died of cancer recently. David loved the sea as he loved the books of Joseph Conrad. David could do anything. And he was probably one of the most charismatic men in the world. His wife, Annette, is equally talented and accomplished, but she doesn't believe she is a whole person without David. Who knows, maybe she isn't? That's my theme: that women need men, the other halves of ourselves. I don't know what I would do without Steel Man, who has made my life so complete and good here in this Midwestern university town.

I think I do believe that we can have these partnerships in spirit as well as in the flesh, though I am sure it is much more difficult. In their beautiful house at Point Dume since David's death, Annette works out that possibility constantly. It is very inspiring to me, though I don't have any idea where she gets the strength for this. It seems almost superhuman.


Yr Lady of Light,


DW

# ON THE TERRACE AT POINT DUME

*Thinking of your blue-shadowed silk,*
*is music.*

Wallace Stevens

The white dome of the house, like an observatory where
        starlight
is measured, allows Mozart to echo through the glass-walled
        room,
and out onto the terrace overlooking the Pacific
where we are having poached salmon under the umbrella.
        It's blue, dark blue, over our heads
        as graceful as night, the ocean inverted,
        into some sailor's eyes.
Once this domed house was only in his mind,
David's concept,
invisible then as he is,
        now that he is dead.
Sailing. He could have been
happy, she said, just sailing his boat,
doing nothing else.

But surfaces were his
pleasure, the shape of this house,
the way the salad of arugula and bibb
or chicory snap at the roof
of the mouth in the balsamic vinaigrette,

150

and seeing the silk
ripple as the water does around your snorkeling tube
exploring a coral reef.
    The Great Barrier,
        a name which offers stars of
            association, spiny sea urchins
                of liquid and pooled innuendo. There is
no
                    wisdom, no solace. It is not that
he is gone, that is not the barrier,
because here at this house he is entirely present.
It is that he, who loved surfaces, no longer has them, and
that we, we who remain, we are all surface;
but he's like the music
echoing off the ceiling. It's not imagination.
If you choose, you can talk to him here
under the surface of this white dome,
    swimming in the blue of ocean, of sky, this worldly
    invisibly starred umbrella where nothing is the
        everything of
music.

---

By dissolving the matter/field distinction, quantum physicists realized a dream of the ancient Greeks who speculated that beneath its varied appearances the world was ultimately composed of a single substance. Some philosophers said it was all Fire; some Water. We now believe the world to be All Quantumstuff.

The world is one substance. As satisfying as this discovery may be to philosophers, it is profoundly distressing to physicists as long as they do not understand the nature of that substance. For if quantumstuff is all there is and you don't understand quantumstuff, your ignorance is complete.

Nick Herbert, *Quantum Reality: Beyond the New Physics*

---

## EMERALDS

He said he dreamed
that a block of ice was after
him. He'd been reading about
anger, and he'd watch a jungle movie
with an invisible enemy.

That same night, lying next to him,
both of us covered with a goose down
comforter, I dreamed that my brother was
an ex-convict, and I was trying to explain to
someone his troubles. I'd been reading
a book about a boy wonder born in Orange
County who made Hollywood blockbuster movies,
and I'd watched a movie about some heroic
kids at a military school who chose to die
for honor.

Drinking coffee in the winter morning,
we saw ice glinting off a bare bush,
the stems seemingly wrapped in glass.
"If your enemy is a block of ice, surely
it will melt," I said.

Later, I went to the video store and rented
*Romancing the Stone.* "Read it and weep,"
the romance writer tells her editor.
One might change one's life for an emerald that
big, that precious. One might also
do terrible things, forsake honor, commit crimes even,
and be convicted.

"This ice didn't melt," he said.
"It was winter during my entire dream."

---

At Moscow University Vladimir Braginski is looking for gravity
waves by monitoring tiny changes in the shape of a 200-pound
sapphire crystal cylinder. Braginski chose this exotic material
because after being struck it continues to quiver for a record
time. Sapphire's long ringing time permits making a maximum
number of measurements before the gravity wave's impact fades
away. To isolate it from terrestrial noise, the Soviet sapphire
is suspended by wires in a vacuum chamber and cooled to near
absolute zero.

Nick Herbert, *Quantum Reality: Beyond the New Physics*

---

# THE SUMMER NUTHATCH SOMETIMES
## HANGS UPSIDE-DOWN

When the basil is greener than emeralds
and has become a bush of leaves bigger than cat's paws
you begin to think of sitting on a beach somewhere,
a puma, black panther, Bengal tiger, smooth-furred,
wearing a silky maillot and a thin gold bracelet.
The book you read is a bankbook, a wallet,
since the pages are like money, a fat chunk of cash
you can leaf through and spend as you like
for a Mont Blanc pen, say, or a box of Belgian chocolates,
the story never disintegrating into insoluble problems.
But the basil
becomes pesto, green and white against the pasta.
Eating it, on the terrace overlooking the ocean,
drinking chardonnay, you know everything is manageable.
You can heal yourself, leaving only a white line of stylish
        scar
where you once were in trouble.
You had
the spirit of a hunter, one of the big cats, and the grace;
your big clawed swipe against snakes or people
kept you alive. This bird, the nuthatch, sometimes
hangs upside-down, just like you did
that summer in Greece where you saw a woman once
sunning herself, nearly naked
on a yacht, her body as beautiful as that of a cougar.

Her emerald bikini against the tanned skin
like basil, like money, like the water of the Mediterranean
in morning light,
or your feelings when you allow yourself
the luxury of connections, or conclusions
    about the Jason with whom you spent that summer
      on a Greek Island.


## UNLIKE STARS


You ask me again and again
why I felt I had no control over my feelings
when plainly, I created them. Unlike stars, or
sparkling wet fish, or the frost patterns
outside on the glass, I form and shape
all the feelings I have, so why did I choose
to love such a hideous man,
more than once in fact, we don't need to name
names, or list their flaws.

There are only secrets hinted at
by the migration of birds,
the famous salmon plunging the weir,
even Lassie Come Home. Well,
here it is, here it is.
The fish that jumps out of the river
—waterstone earrings scattering across my cheek—
is radiating color. His eye
passes the test, the one I never
could.

You might as well accept
that it's all stories, all parallel
universes with different outcomes,
that observers create it all,
that I put the frost on the window,
the salmon decided he wanted to climb a certain ladder,
and I was asking, just asking
for trouble, blaming biology
when in fact I decided
to live the stories, rather than just
to read them.

The Rose Diner

Dear Craig,

"This is the way to change the past," says Nick
Herbert, explaining an experiment in quantum physics
which leads one to the conclusion that the way you
think about an event in retrospect actually is part of a
retroactive deciding process. I suppose this fits into all
the revisionist history which Feminists and other
scholars of diversity are currently proposing. I've
discovered, however, that most physicists despite these
"poetic" interpretations of their theories about space,
time, motion, think of these things mechanically.
Maybe the words "poetic" and "creative" should both
be eliminated from current vocabulary. We seem only
to debase ourselves with them.

I've been reading an excellent new book by Jeremy Bernstein called *Quantum Profiles,* thinking more about how poetic ideas of the universe have evolved. He doesn't have much use for the way non-scientists think about quantum theory. In fact, he ridicules quotations from literary sources for about a page in his introductory chapter about John Stewart Bell, finishing with this *coup de grace:*

While most physicists would find these capsule descriptions of the quantum theory caricatural, there is enough truth in them to explain why people who seem to have an aversion to more conventional science are drawn to the quantum theory. The quantum theory has become the basis of the New Age outlook, with its emphasis on Eastern religions and holistic medicine. This surely would have astonished Oppenheimer, who, incidentally, studied Sanskrit so that he could read the *Upanishads* in the original. Books like Gary Zukav's *The Dancing Wu Li Masters* — quantum theory with a dash of Eastern mysticism — abound, and no ashram — at least, no Western one — can afford to be without its resident expert. Just recently, in a health food store in Greenwich Village, I came across an announcement in the *I Am News* of the Ananda Ashram in Monroe, New York, which, under the heading "Quantum Dynamics," reads, "Spiritual Purification Program, includes meditation, fire ceremony, rebirthing, sweat lodge and Quantum Dynamics

initiation for those who haven't had it; includes breathing tech-
niques and mantra to dissolve upsets. This weekend we will
work with Quantum Dynamics to dissolve past life karma all
the way back to original cause."
*Pace,* Robert Oppenheimer.

Jeremy Bernstein, Quantum Profiles

---

Indeed, I am put in my place. Change the past in-
deed! How poetic and non-scientific. Though I must
say I don't like *The Dancing Wu Li Masters* any better
than Bernstein does. The battle between the scientists
and humanists seems unending. Too bad. We might
really fix up the world if we could stop quarreling. In
the old days I was lumped with the Feminists to take
away the seriousness of my poetry. Now, I guess I'll
be lumped into New Age pap. Oh, Diane, rewrite
your history, your life.

Forget that for a while, Craig. Here's a paradox for
you. About the word "quantum." People say "he
took a quantum leap," meaning infinite or so large
you can't measure it. But that is the exact opposite of
what quantum actually means. Quantum really refers
to the fact that you can quantify or measure
something. So a quantum leap is a measurable leap.
Actually, I think it originally referred to a very very
small measurement.

Of course, one of the points from which quantum theory proceeds is the notion that the instant you measure something, that act of measuring changes the thing; thus the process of learning or knowing always itself seems to obscure/change the original (or pure) thing measured. I've spent so many years thinking about whether or not my life could have been any different than it has been. Had I been born beautiful, I wonder, or rich, what would my life have been? Has all this measuring changed it? I remain in quantum ignorance,

Yr Lady of East Lansing,

DW

---

Just as quantum ignorance is different from the classical kind, the "knowledge" that we gain in a quantum measurement is of a different sort from the knowledge we gain from opening an envelope.

Nick Herbert, *Quantum Reality: Beyond the New Physics*

---

# T'AI CHI

The tips of the lilac bush show
around the edge of the blue spruce,
and they are tight plumes of raspberry-juiced bud knots,
still furled against early grey spring, not yet the color
we designate true American "lilac." I make the distinction
against the French breed, which remain a richer
color. Maybe I don't know what I'm
talking about, maybe the idea of
observer-created reality
doesn't mean the same thing
to a scientist and someone who's not,
but why ridicule someone who wants to understand
the universe, who values poetry even if she doesn't know
what it is, why despise her for talking about a physics
she can't pass a test in. American education, said one
researcher, over-emphasizes testing, creates
specialization (i.e. vocabulary) in place of understanding
        the basics,
seeing the bigger picture. There is something wrong with
not being able to speak more than one language,
or feeling that the only way you could learn anything
is in school. The lilac buds, at this time of year, seem like
decoration rather than substance. Like knowing a foreign
        language
only so that you could visit expensive restaurants with more
sophistication.

160

She looks unhealthy when I see her for lunch
once a month. I know she has more problems than
just her desire to be perfect, her inability some days
to even talk through a door to another person. I see only
the tips of her bush, her lilac bud self. Know even the color
will change as the season progresses. It is the T'ai Chi figure
      eight I
do
over and over, pushing my legs, my arms, my whole torso
into infinity or the sense of its possibility. Even for
ten minutes it seems to connect me to something
from which I normally am excluded
a language I can finally understand,
though perhaps not yet speak.

## WHITE CARDAMOM

*for Norman Hindley*

What were you doing
with the woman whose lips
are the first thing I think of when her
name
is mentioned? Didn't you
understand the rituals between men
and women?

That the Lady
must say no, must establish her

161

purity, must keep her life chaste,
must be as white as those beautiful cardamom seeds
you sent to me, for crushing into my Indian-style
tea?

Didn't you know what every Knight
must know; that your loyalty is required? Not that
misinterpretation of chivalric code: "no means yes."

No doesn't
mean yes. No means
no, not yet.
You haven't proven your
loyalty yet,
you haven't given enough yet,
you haven't earned love
yet, or favors, or troth
                    (translate that to "truth"?)

So, what I want to know is
what were you doing with the woman who never
said no?

I bought a small soft cup of whole black cardamom seeds
one day, before you sent me the white ones. My shop
          didn't carry
those pearly nuggets. But twisting the black cardamom in
          my mortar
didn't yield that fresh aroma that is like no other. The
          black seeds
were tough, like roots, stringy rather than brittle, not perfect
for infusions, or perfect for marrying their fresh healthy
          aroma
with spidery Darjeeling leaves. Didn't you see

that she was like the black cardamom. Yes, she said,
but it's the white, the pure white seeds which enhance
the tea.

I think you knew this, or you wouldn't have sent me
the gift, four or five years later, but the trope, the figure,
is sometimes
substitute for the ground. I share my cup of
tea with the Knight who understands what yes
really means, who waits through no, and no, and no, and
        does not
misinterpret either figure or ground, sends me jewels I
cannot wear. He understands yes. He accepts no.
We both have thin lips and elaborate ceremonies. We never
        read
yes as no or no as yes; we too find your Lady's camellia lips
attractive, but she will always say yes when she means
no, and vice versa.

I don't even offer her a cup
of morning tea. And I never understood why you did.
I thought you knew white cardamom from black.
I thought you understood the code.


## SATIN


Her hands were never beautiful, but they
felt nice, like satin. She became
a lesbian; she became a political radical;

163

she became a philosopher; she never stopped
biting her nails.

Why don't you look her up, and old friend
chides me. She'd love to hear from you after all
these years. So would a lot of other people, I think.
So would a lot of other people. But what,
I ask myself, makes me even think of looking
them up. They were never people I liked; they
were people whom I thought, with a little help, could
become people I'd like or be interested in.

Maybe I should have become a sculptor
rather than a poet. Plato was right, poets
are liars, and you can't shape
people
with words; even more impossible to re-
make them
with language. Why should I
want to? Words are only materials.
Useless materials
when you haven't the tools to use them.

I still remember looking at those end-bitten hands
of a college roommate and thinking that
they seemed so smooth and might be
like satin, they might be hands which drew lovers,
if they were tipped with long oval nails, shiny
with blood red lacquer, delicate points
to draw you into her needs. But her bloody points
were elsewhere; her hands only a symbol,
not the failures themselves. I suppose
I should call her some time, though I suspect
even having a cup of tea with this woman would draw
my eyes to her hands, and I'd only feel one thing:

disapproval. Some say the eyes are the mirrors to
you know what. I say the hands. When you visit me,
wear gloves if you don't want my eyes
to write your history, wrap you up and yes,
throw you away. Look at my own hands:
claws, as I age. Little claws.


## A CLOAK OF FOLDED WINGS


I wondered
when she told me how she
loved to garden
and how impossible it was with the
tall elms shading her backyard
to make anything grow there, why she didn't
think of having them trimmed
at least.

I wondered
when she told me how she
loved to cook
and found that her stove had only one
working burner on it
why she didn't call Appliance Technicians
or at least a local handyman.

I wondered
when she told me how she
wanted to be an actress

why she stopped going to the theater,
even though
she lived in New York City.

I wondered why
I was listening to her,
at a certain point,
why I had become so still,
like one of those hand-sized blue butterflies
pinned against cotton wool, behind glass
in the Natural History museum

                                   she was
talking to me because she thought I was rare, was beautiful,
she knew I would understand, would see her as someone
        with
brilliant wings, gold veined, antennae of black velvet,
wanting to fly over the Andes.

I was thinking all the while
that I wished I could be playing
a slot machine, putting in coin after coin
hoping to see four sevens, the red
appearing against the white
not as a signal of distress but as
the wedding spot of scarlet on the Sicilian white sheet
hanging out over the balcony the next morning.

I was thinking that she
was the butterfly and I was
the caterpillar/I had images of
those dusty tents of web the Gypsy moths
put into blighted trees; of Miss Havisham and the movie
version of her cobwebby house, silver as tinsel;

the wedding dress molded, white satin never used
decays just as surely as white stain, stained
from a night of dancing, champagne, bowered love.

I was thinking that she
couldn't see inside my head, with its own
cobwebs of age and that she was opening her mouth
not her mind or her life, but oddly I did not want
her to stop talking, for fear that then
I might be required to say something. Sitting here
looking at the drifting particles of snow against my tall
       bare oak
trees
in Michigan, I fantasize the things I might have said
which could have changed my life in so many
different conversations, wondering if at the time
they all seemed as meaningless, or vain,
or wasteful, as this woman's monologue.

Silence has been my rock. You might
think of engraving that some day
when there's a final reason for my reticence.
We know I am not a woman
dreaming of a butterfly, though I suppose
I could be a butterfly
dreaming of a woman, one who would be silent
as a cloak of folded wings.

# DAWN BUDS

How could her paintings
like a hundred butterfly silk scarves folded
into a cedar drawer be anything
but decoration?

Yet you might think
that all she wore was scarves,
no underwear, no stockings, no blouse,
dress or trouser/only scarves draped over her body,
thus so many of them folded into the cedar drawer.

On the desert where one doesn't think
of silk, unless it is raw, pebbly as sand,
a cloth for nuns or anchorites, this woman
could live and it would only be
when you looked at her paintings,
particularly her paintings of flowers,
that you would realize
decoration
wasn't trivial,
an accessory,
a scarf, draped tastefully
over the shoulder.

You might think of her as a child on the prairie,
or an old woman wearing a black hat on the desert,
but you could never stop wondering about the drawerful
of poppy red, orchid pink, pansy blue, datura white
scarves, the phalanopsis, moth-winged floating cloth
of her imagination, flying out of the drawer.
You would always love this beauty.

She moved to the desert
and even there
found flowers to be substantial,
not just decoration. Especially there,
so much so, she no longer needed
to paint them, or is it that they turned into
skulls of animals, like scarves
of cartilage, the desert itself a drawerful
of silky bones?

# ZURBARAN

A brilliant painter, he was skillful in effects
of color and light . . . His interest in the
real world is evident in the pleasure he
takes in reproducing the turquoise or violet
of silk satins, the thick red velvets, and the
rich colorful embroideries and the heavy
white habits of the monks as well as in his
evocation of the Andalusian grace and
beauty of his "female saints," or the fruits,
flowers, and the terra cottas of his still
lifes.

*from a catalogue*


It is light
which defines
the real world.

And yet dermatologists advise us
that prolonged light on the skin produces
damage. In fact, says the Lady Dermatologist on the
talk show, any tan is a sign of damaged cells.
The callers keep saying that light
on the skin is healthy,
that tanning is protection,
she smiles with her voice and says

"tanning is better
than burning. Both are signs of
damaged cells." Only the pure color of birth skin, she
reminds them, is the healthy colour; the only pigmentation
healthy, the one your birth race equipped you with.

Lady D., whom I've never seen, but who sounds as if
she has milky skin, slightly freckled from birth with some
Irish genes, soothes each caller, mentioning how good
the sun-screen products are. She also reminds the farm
        worker
his skin will tan with prolonged exposure in the sun.
That's part of his job. Wear protective clothing, buy sun-
screen. They hang up.

No caller will give up the idea
that light on the skin is healthy. That children
need to play in the sunshine, but the doctor,
Lady D. jollies them along, yes tan is better than burn,
yes, there is Vitamin D in the sunlight, but any skin
different from that you were born with
is damaged.

No one gets angry with her.
I smile as I am driving, thinking that living itself
is damage, the older we grow the less healthy our cells are.

A doctor once told me that when he was in medical school
the students would look at a cadaver and pronounce often
        that a
body had "PPP."

What's that?

"Piss Poor Protoplasm."

171

Usually the old. Usually the
diseased. He recounted a man whom he had treated in his
        practice
who survived being in cold sea water past the point of
        hypothermia.
His protoplasm was in great shape. Even slight exposure to
        such
for most is death. The more so, if you have
"PPP."

The paint offers
the heavy drape of rich fabrics
and the way the light plays
on the silky textures,
but the light positively radiates
out of the white habits his monks wear.
They serve their faith. They serve god. They serve
also the painter.

Have you noticed how many of his paintings have black
backgrounds? In fact, all
that I've viewed.
Out of darkness, comes light?
Silly cliché, obvious observation.
But the blackness
against which the white skins of his rich women,
or his table vessels in the still lifes
or the robes of the virginal men
rest — that is what
the painter must create in order
to define his reality.

I have so wanted
in this life to believe
"amor vincit omnia."

I should have learned from my Southern California childhood
that lights both flatter and reveal every wrinkle.
Hollywood puts the flood lights on love,
but against a background of dark secrets
and human failures, the stars twist and turn like the
        hanged man,
glinting in the orange grove.

Reich claimed that over the graves of the newly buried
there was detected radiation of the kind he called "blue
        bions."
Hounded to death, not more than a little crazy, he and his
observations can easily be written off, ignored, but
what if this protoplasm IS light? What if there is only
LOSS of light?

Love, then, becomes irrelevant
until translated. The woman holding the edge of her
umber gown, teal blue sleeve draped and glistening with
        water light
against her ocher and yellow bustled cape, called "St.
        Elizabeth of Portugal"
by the painter, she is white in the hands and neck, the mask
        of face,
he shows. Her hair black as the background.
He would have loved painting Elizabeth Taylor had he lived
        past
1664.

Lady D. on the "Meet the Dermatologist" show
says again, in her pink tulip voice,
"any darkening of the skin shows damaged cells."

Different from its natural pigmentation she means.

She's giving me mixed messages,
for enduring darkness is what you must learn.
To survive. It's what you must face
when you die. It's
what makes us able to use light.
Her truth—that light is death.

How do I learn that
in a world where love
is darkness,
and I long for light?

## IMAGINING EMILY'S
## EARLY SUMMER GARDEN

I heard June Jordan tell a poetry class that
she had little use for Emily Dickinson (this was
when she was describing herself as a "daughter
of Walt Whitman" poetically) because she'd
heard that during the Civil War a group of
slaves had sent quilts that they had made to
groups of New Englanders in gratitude for
their help with the emancipation and that
Emily Dickinson had used the one she received
as a ground cloth to put under her knees when
she was gardening.

To Jordan, this seemed the disdainful act of a
white supremacist. To me, it seemed like a
religious act, kneeling on the quilt as she
worked in the earth with her own hands which
expressed the commonality and grounding in
the Dionysian, earthy world they all shared,
slave and master. Perhaps simply one difference
between the way whites and blacks might in-
terpret history and literature.


Scarlet poppies with their
                    coal centers, eye-
                              lashed and vulnerable
as the petals wash, flop off,
                    and lie discarded
                              are taller
than the peonies this year,
                    though they've
                              inhabited that ground
only half
                    as long. I planted the seeds indoors
                              a few years ago,
nursed them along,
                    the plants
                              now are nubby and
tough and one remembers old gardeners talking
                    of how wild and hardy
                              they can be.
I kneeled last year in another corner
                    of the garden
                              with a new set
of seedling poppies
                    which got a small dainty hold,
                              each offering one

175

pastel bloom
                    before autumn.
                                I assumed they'd
return,
but they were not there
                    this spring.
                                When I kneel before
my plants, I never know
                    which ones will be tough enough
                                to survive. Or
whether, if
they do, they'll blossom.
                    So hard to imagine anyone
                                envying, or
despising, Emily Dickinson. Hate must come
                    in categories, to do such a thing.
                                She held so much
close
And shared pain only
                    with the earth, I think.
                                Perhaps only an
urban
woman could see contempt
                    in kneeling on the lovingly
                                stitched quilt,
some one who never put her hands
                    in the earth, her white hands
                                which then came
out black and common, the quilt
                    which like a prayer rug
                                signaled and
shared the sacred nature of her task.

# OLD GARDEN

I examine
over my pearly silent keyboard,
a glove of oak leaves caught
in the blue spruce, a snake of green garden hose
still looped through the grey slats of the fence,
the elderly juniper bushes like straggly old horses.
A rosebush is my mother and all my failed lovers.

The trope. I talk about the trope;
it's the key, a figure against the ground.
The birds make metaphors,
while I imagine flying to each port
of the feeder,
twirling in the wind, taking a seed in my beak
and cracking it as I sail away
always with Jason, the betrayer,
the sailor of my dreamlight.

# WHAT OTHERS HEAR

She is drinking water from a thick blue glass goblet,
and wondering how you ever rid the world of any system
which allows people, like the Aztecs, to cut out each other's
        hearts,
and wondering why she thinks that when she sets the
        glass down
she might discover that it has a little and very deadly
        snake,
like a Coral, coiling in it, ready to kill her.
She wonders why she behaves so badly, so often,
when all she wants, all she believes in
is order, clean sheets, control that comes from
moderation, restraint, simplicity,
not pain or deprivation, and certainly not
perversity.

But she knows that when others watch her
holding the blue glass goblet in her short fingered
ringless hand, and when they hear her speaking her irritation
at the irrational, and her contempt at the stupid or cruel,
they hear the very snake she fears, that little Coral whip
invisible, shy perhaps/just not wanting to be disturbed,
venomous when anything touches its smoothness.

No one believes she only drinks water from that glass,
some think it contains a drug, others that she is sustained

only on pure poison. They are the ones who think she drives
    people
insane, avoid her in public, and privately describe her
as the snake she herself so fears.

There is nothing, nothing,
she can do,
to change this. She lies awake
at night sometimes, wondering where
she went wrong, what made her actions seem
so cruel to some and so crude or taboo
to others. She is not even sure what those actions were/are
any more, for all she remembers is the blue glass goblet,
her hand holding it, and the fact that she is terrified
by darkness, that night has always seemed to be a time
when she could scream and scream,
and no one would hear her.
Or perhaps
    as if sound were the snake hidden in night's blue glass
goblet,
they would hear something different. A hiss.
A hissing, like steam rising from the glass.
And though they might hear,
they would never come to her aid.

# STILL THINKING OF ORCHIDS

The green python looked like a succulent,
    a kind of cactus flower-curled against its rainy wall,
        and who could imagine a garden without a snake?

Jeffers
    saw God walking over a stormy Point Sur in the form
        of lightning,
In lightning he'd walk,
    just as Stevens' lion would become light
        and walk—is it into? or out of?—
a glass of water
    reflecting a gloved hand,
        a hawk.

I know that there could be a moment
    in time when we'd find all the stories converging,
        and then we'd have a crusty loaf of bread,
the ocean's salty air on our lips, the moon
    would turn into a phalanopsis,
        and fly over us.

This play would have no villains
    and everyone would wear the mask
    of a flower.

Cymbidium,
    the name of a character in a play.


        She could be a
Ginger
        blossom. Plumaria


        I wonder if my own love
of white-painted adobe houses,
    orchids cascading from terra cotta jars on their patios, isn't
        an unwillingness to accept Eastern gardens,

                                                        snakes?

                                The Rose Diner

Dear Craig,

This is what I have been chewing on for the past few
days. Why/how to come to terms with the fact that
living one's life seems to consist of plans for the
future rather than being in the present? It's always
what you are going to do with your life, rather than
what you are doing with it. I suppose I see a lopsided
version of the world, with so many young people
passing always in front of me.

I am disturbed by the fact that you don't see your
current job or education as meaningful in the bigger
picture of your life. Of course this is a woman talking
whose life ended before she even began to feel she
lived it.

# THE CHALKBOARD

It's as if it were a map
spreading across the long wall of my office,
showing a world of green, which if the earth were really
flat, we'd all fall off the edge
onto, this place of summer-leafed infinity.
Other tenants of these offices have requested the removal
of the blackboards which, in these rooms, must represent
      the fact
that classes once were taught here. But I cannot bring
      myself to
make this request, some part of me loves
seeing this expanse of slate, yes a dull green,
but nature's greens can be quite dull as well, for instance
the autumn garden I look out on this morning, the oaks
      still cloaked
with dusty summer leaves, the floor of foliage from spring's
      lilies-of
the-valley dulling before they dry out and brown, the locust
      tree
which Steel Man trimmed back yesterday losing its vibrancy.

My chalkboard
on which I've written nothing, could be my life, but more
      than that
it reminds me that words and numbers present so many
      possibilities,

that failing is to fall off the edge of one world and
        underneath
is this expanse of sultry green where, if you wish, you
        can write
the same numbers or words and try again to make a
        constellation
that others could perceive, as you see it, maybe my name
        "Diane"
or the word "arrow," or "huntress," "chaste/chased," "the
        moon," and
the number "nineteen," or "three";

they might shine down on the world
bringing light from a million years ago.

---

Well, if only we knew at the beginning that nothing
is possible unless some definition of self is accepted and
believed. I have always believed I was special and that
whatever I chose in life would be special too. For in-
stance, I have never questioned the importance of
poetry, probably because I chose poetry. And yet I
always feel that before I can talk to anyone else about
poetry, I have to establish its authenticity. An authen-
ticity I myself never questioned. I am sure I don't
understand this. Could it be like star-light, which
might no longer exist by the time it reaches the earth?

Yr Lady of Star Light,

DW

# STARRY, STARRY, WINDOWS
## OF THE SOUL?

Steel Man, who photographs people's eyes unflinchingly,
won his second Nikon in a contest called "The Eyes of
      Laura Mars."
In the dappled light of the Ala Moana Shopping Mall in
      Honolulu, he
carried his photo
of a friend's teenage daughter.
Her eyes looked right at you, a chef selecting mercilessly
the most perfect eggplant, a smoothskinned fat bulb,
the sweetest onion, and three tomatoes whose skin will
      curl away
for taut ripeness.

Like the fashion photographer who saw
what one man longed to slash out,
she looks from the photo slightly amused at perfect
surfaces, and subtle blemishes.

The photographer seems to know
that eyes do not record surfaces only,
and the eyes of his portrait subjects, they seem
always to be cutting away, and cutting away, at onion-
      like layers
of surfacing. The deep reality, the core,
it is light itself

184

and one feels, especially in his women,
—the sibyls, Delphic oracle priestesses or Martian women—
that they are reading the future
because they are molding it.

With their eyes,
they tell you,
this soft lavender bell will become
the shiny eggplant, and this yellow star
the tomato. Under the juicy green spike is the
ball with its crackling envelope like an airmail letter
and my hands someday
will skin these vegetables long after
these eyes did it originally.

When you think you are looking into someone's eyes
what is really happening is that they are pushing you
          back
into your own core where you recognize
a message which is always the same at the root.
Light. Everything is made of light.
You only imagine there are windows framing it.

---

What's at stake in the quantum reality question is not the ac-
tual existence of electrons but *the manner in which electrons possess
their major attributes.* Classical physicists imagined that every par-
ticle possessed at each moment a definite position and momen-
tum; each field likewise possessed a particular field strength at
every location. If we agree to call any entity—particle, field,
apple, or galaxy—which possesses its attributes innately an

"ordinary object" then the fundamental message of classical physics was this: the entire physical world consists of nothing but ordinary objects.

Nick Herbert, *Quantum Reality: Beyond the New Physics*

# ORDINARY OBJECTS/COILS OF BEAUTY

There were the oranges
which always intrigued me,
that faint blush of green near the buttoned disc
connecting stem to fruit, and the dusting
of earth which had settled over the top curve of the fruit,
fresh from the morning tree.
And the apricots which fell off their seeds
into a ragged dark jam on the orchard floor, drawing
the bees, whose velvet bodies I loved as a child.

I remember the first apple I ate. I was
twelve. A new roadside stand/
East Whittier, home of MFK Fisher whom I had not yet
        heard of/
Washington Delicious apples, crisp as ice,
the first crack of flesh
that made me forever know
fresh apples really came
from Paradise, and it wasn't Southern California

which was too hot and dry to grow
good ones. Birds of Paradise, but not apples
were in this garden.

I have no early memory of exotic fruits,
but grapes are there, early. Their scent, the smell
of purple, their name Concord, meaning peace
or Massachusetts, and their identity
connected to an arbor over a backyard sidewalk
which was always dark, even in the heat of summer afternoons,
and the fragrance wrapped around your head
as those tendrils of grapevine wound greenly, like coils
of beauty, clinging to any hold.

The woman who took care of us
after school and walked up Santa Fe Springs Road
with her shopping bags each afternoon,
the paper permeated with the smell of Juicy Fruit chewing gum
and cherry Lifesavers. What was her name? she is
my image for the phrase "Bag Lady," but she was a Sugar
        Lady,
heavy and plump and rosy, sugar which displaced the sweetness
of those real fruits, and she taught me about silver foil
        wrapped
things
which never spoiled, like gum and candy.
But there had to be a garden
where the real fruits never spoiled either because,
as it said in my fairy tales, the fruits were made
of ruby, emerald, diamond, sapphire, or chunks of gold,
and I grew up to believe that fruit should not
go soft or spoil and decay,
to savor dried figs, sugary desert-ripened dates,
and never to stop searching for tightly crisp apple flesh

which when I find, I eat
with cheeses, soft and hard,
and thick crusted bread.

I will never give up my glass of red wine,
for that is the final fruit which does not spoil, its
fermentation only ages it into glory and cellared pleasure.

When I grew up my house was innocent of carpets, vacuum
        cleaners,
real silverware, crystal goblets or even a corkscrew. My
        mother
was a bookkeeper and I was a bookworm,
and fruit was outside my backdoor,
even when there was little other beauty
coiling in my desert life.

---

Quantum theory suggests, on the other hand, that the world
is *not* made of ordinary objects. An electron, and every other
quantum entity, does not possess all its attributes innately. An
electron does not possess certain innate attributes — mass, charge,
and spin, for instance — which serve to distinguish it from other
kinds of quantum entities. The value of these attributes is the
same for every electron under all measurement conditions. With
respect to these particular attributes, even the electron behaves
like an ordinary object.

Nick Herbert, *Quantum Reality: Beyond the New Physics*

# WINDOW MOON

At just the moment of apogee,
like a white boulder fallen from one of
those mountains in the Sierras where Rexroth
liked going camping,
its circumference nearly filled
the window on the bedroom roof-door.

At just that moment I must
have dreamed something like a huge flower,
a white datura trumpet perhaps,
hovering over my face, blowing into my ear,
brushing against my eyebrows.

And just at that moment
I woke up, almost felt I could
talk to the moon, its face was pressing so urgently
into the window, the light giving me a sense
of presence rather than illumination.

The moon as large
as a hubcap and I no longer the sleeper,
the room still dark, my husband still sailing his dreamship,
but that big white canvas sail of a moon outside the window
seemed to be flapping at me. As bright
as the moon was, it
shed very little light into the room.

Downstairs there were
the white phalanopsis flowers,
the moth orchids,
blooming,
an image of beauty which somehow represents me better
than my old snail body, which is still fat in its shell
but leaves less of a trail of slime
on the leaves each day. The moon
in my window tonight
urging me out of bed
to go down and look at the orchids.

## PORTRAIT OF A LADY

The fullness,
Spring's white petalled ocean
of branches/Dr/Swing,
until they are scattered. Sheets of
paper on which the poems swirl
like the waves at Point Dume. I'll come to
your rescue, he said,
like Odysseus, I said, or Lancelot/
then you'll put me in a story.

What's wrong with that?
How can a story be anything but heroic
the way
I write it?

He seemed to think that the swing
of petals, their flurry,
could only scatter his parts, am I some
Maenad, I asked, but he obviously didn't
want to answer.

Swing flowers, the apple blossoms which scatter
their instantly old petals, oh swing, swing,
but he never knew that I thought he was a hero, just
had an image of papers blowing,
scattered over the ocean, like petals.

## JASON THE BETRAYER

Withdrawing the wisteria,
    her trailing arms
    in silk kimonoed whiteness,
and seeing the grape-like cluster
of blossom hidden by
all the clothes in the closet/you
        don't even know what it means to keep
    a secret, you don't know how important it is
            to offer distractions, false clues, sometimes even
imply a lie, if not actually tell one.

I too like the image of the glacier
holding the greenness I see right now
in the heavy foliage on our wisteria vine,
the thicket of oak leaves screening our back garden
from the neighbors' houses and driveways.

191

And of the bones caught in this stiff water
from the past, the idea of lives caught up
and preserved as if for our inspection.

The ice axe frightens me a little. Both ends
of the blade so sharp. Tools have never been something
I desired to hold in my hand, but to look at them, gleaming
and new, especially in the hardware store, with its faint smell
of metal filings and oil, and an assortment of harsh cleaning
compounds,
offers one of the many glimpses of the male world which
intrigues me. I would have been the little girl who
sat in Daddy's lap while he drank beer with his
cronies and watched football on TV.

This wisteria vine covers everything including its own
          blossoms.
Why do I think there is something I do not know about
hidden there? A few weeks ago, it was all bare skinny bark
and twisting tough wood. Nothing hidden, not even the
          secret of
its strength which allows it to crush the slats of our fence
in its snaky curl. So why do I think now that it is hiding
some truth about my life, or men, my father, any Jason I
might have known? This seems an act of will. The woman
in the silk kimono. What does she see out my windows
when I am looking in my mind, out beyond the oaks,
pretending that I see the Pacific Ocean? Grey with foamy
          white
crests on a stormy day like this one.
Blue like silk on other days,
showing a bit of pale white-fleshed arm
at the throat and cuff.

# MEDEA'S CHARIOT

No one is with me,
    driving the highway into sparc Wyoming
    in this car
    which holds me impersonally, the way a movie star
    holds another actor,
    and makes me think of how I look
    behind the wheel,
    a woman in her late thirties,
    tanned and gleaming with American beef
    and fresh vegetables.

    I wear driving gloves, short bits of pigskin
    with their little pucks of elegance,
    snaps at the wrist, and my arms are slim
    suspended like fuschia stamen over the wheel
    of my brown Audi.

What bad eyes see
    is silhouettes, and we have
    memorized details to go with those shapes
    which are radiantly acute.
    So, though it seems improbable
    with my thick disguising aviator glasses,
    I do notice the hawks that sit on telephone poles
    or the staves of prairie fence.
    I do see the rivulets on breast

or the fan of redtail,
I do remark the shape or pattern of crow or raven
in contrast to vulture, eagle or hawk.

The road leads me, like a rattlesnake
curving in rhythmic undulations,
the hiss of my tires singing me
away from apple trees and cherries,
to Yellowstone and buffalo,
to geysers, to the Tetons
that only look like decorations.

I never forget
there was a Jason.
I never forget fleeing
from California and the West
beyond snake worship
to the magic language of riddles
and spells.

I know that I left
the garden of Orange County
with only three of those golden fruit
in my wallet, and when I return to Las Vegas
I pull and pull the handles of machines,
trying to line up cherries or oranges or plums
whenever I can.

I tell you though, no
sorcery will save you from
the major rules, and if
it seems to, then you have only
misread them, mis-heard
them.

Aeneas is supposed to return,
    golden bough or not, and Medea
    to escape despite fratricide, infanticide.
    Stories cannot be compared quantitatively.
    No fairness ever
    if you compare how much
    or how long or
    who gets what. The rules
    are about the patterns, the stories,
    completing the cycles or rhythms.

As any gambler can tell you,
    if you bet on either patterns or randomness
    you lose. What you have to observe
    is completion, and usually not a big enough sample
    is possible, ever to see it. So

    you are radiant when you win
    and silent
    when you don't. You
    never lose sight of something
    diurnal, a rhythm perhaps, or a
    story.

Following this road
    in America, which is empty of everything
    but my car and the hawks
    on the fence posts, is the quest.
    Not even dreaming yet
    there are other seekers
    on this empty road.

# LONG-STEMMED

He said he could hear the flowers
sighing like women
in their green florist-paper
dressing gowns,
and I thought
that there might be a woman who had flowers
rather than feet,
there might be a world without prisons,
where you offered your hand, a lily,
and there would not be blood.

She on her balcony in emerald silk.
This morning with summer eyes
saying good-bye.

# AMARYLLIS

So seldom
do I see myself that way,
the trumpet as red as a satin garter,
the petals like bedroom walls
or the membrane-thin shade of a bedside lamp,
a spiky head with a rouged mouth singing oratorios
or cantatas, waxy-voiced, the candle in
the window, on a snowy winter
night.

\* \* \*

Printed May 1993 in Santa Barbara & Ann
Arbor for the Black Sparrow Press by Mackintosh
Typography & Edwards Brothers Inc.
Text set in Bembo by Words Worth.
Design by Barbara Martin.
This edition is published in paper wrappers;
there are 300 hardcover trade copies;
125 copies have been numbered & signed
by the poet; & 26 lettered copies with an
original holograph poem have been handbound
in boards by Earle Gray & are signed by the poet.

Photo: Robert Turney

DIANE WAKOSKI was born in Whittier, California in 1937 and educated at U.C., Berkeley. She has published nineteen full-length collections of poems and many other slim volumes. Her two most recent collections from Black Sparrow are *Emerald Ice: Selected Poems 1962–1987* (1988) which won the Poetry Society of America's William Carlos Williams Award in 1988, and *Medea the Sorceress* (1990). She is currently Writer in Residence at Michigan State University.

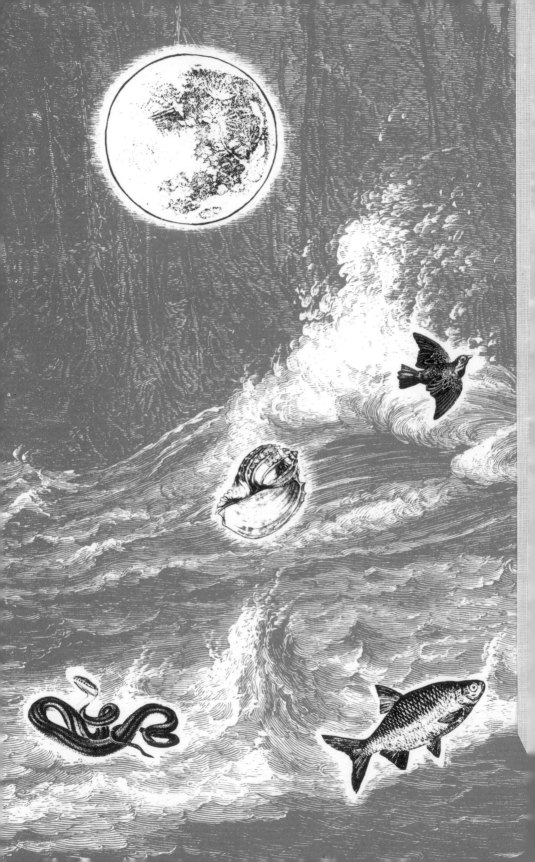